Scottish Crafts Now

'Crafts as artistic statements are created in free space — the best are ideas made into objects for the use of the mind, objects which could not be realised without the skills of craftsmanship'.
Max Bill

'The role of the craftsman is to create an environment of useable yet beautiful objects'.
Carl Auboch

'Discipline of the intellect for its own sake has become an escape from reality. It is not theory that produces progress but rather, the doing. Craftsmen both design and manufacture, solving problems as they go along, not working by a set of preconceived set of instructions'.
Patrick Nuttgens

Excerpts from Keynote lectures:
World Crafts Council Conference, Vienna 1980

'A craftsman is one who can give a physical presence to the strange and beautiful results of imagination, so that what would not exist but for one person's vision and dexterity becomes available to others for their use and their delight; and if the imagination and the skill are of a high enough order there is something magical in the result'.

Robert Gooden
Chairman, Crafts Council

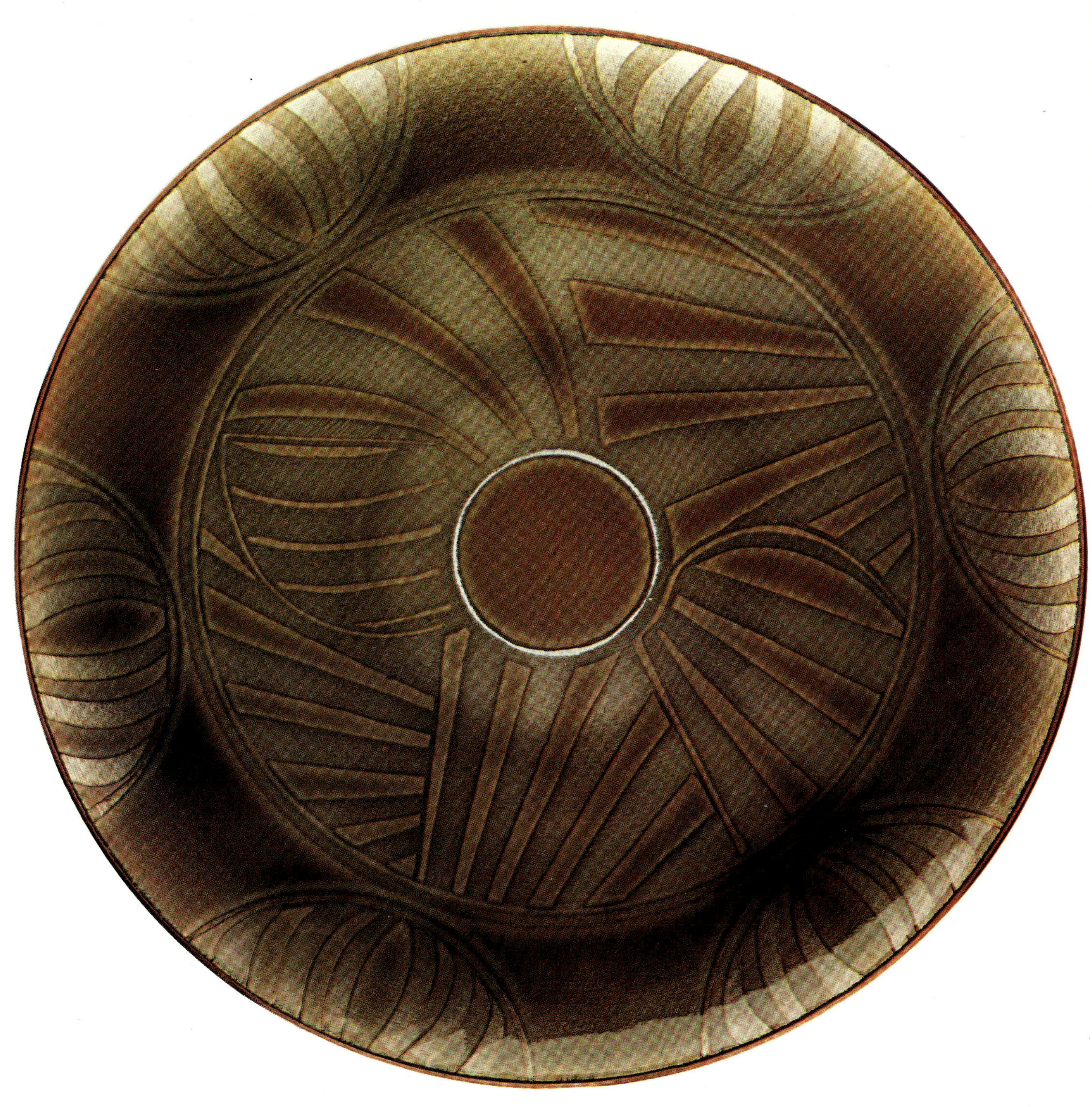

Robin Banks
Enamelled dish
Industrially spun copper dish shape sprayed with
backing enamel and fired concurrently with top
glazes at 800-850°C. Five firings required. The
incised designs below the surface have a
relationship to Mexican plate designs.
The dish is part of a collection of Scottish
Craftwork owned by the Scottish Development
Agency.
39.5 cm diameter

Scottish Crafts Now

published by
Scottish Development Agency
Small Business Division
102 Telford Road
Edinburgh EH4 2NP
©Scottish Development Agency 1980
ISBN 0 905574 02 8

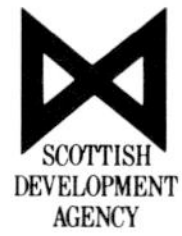

Contents

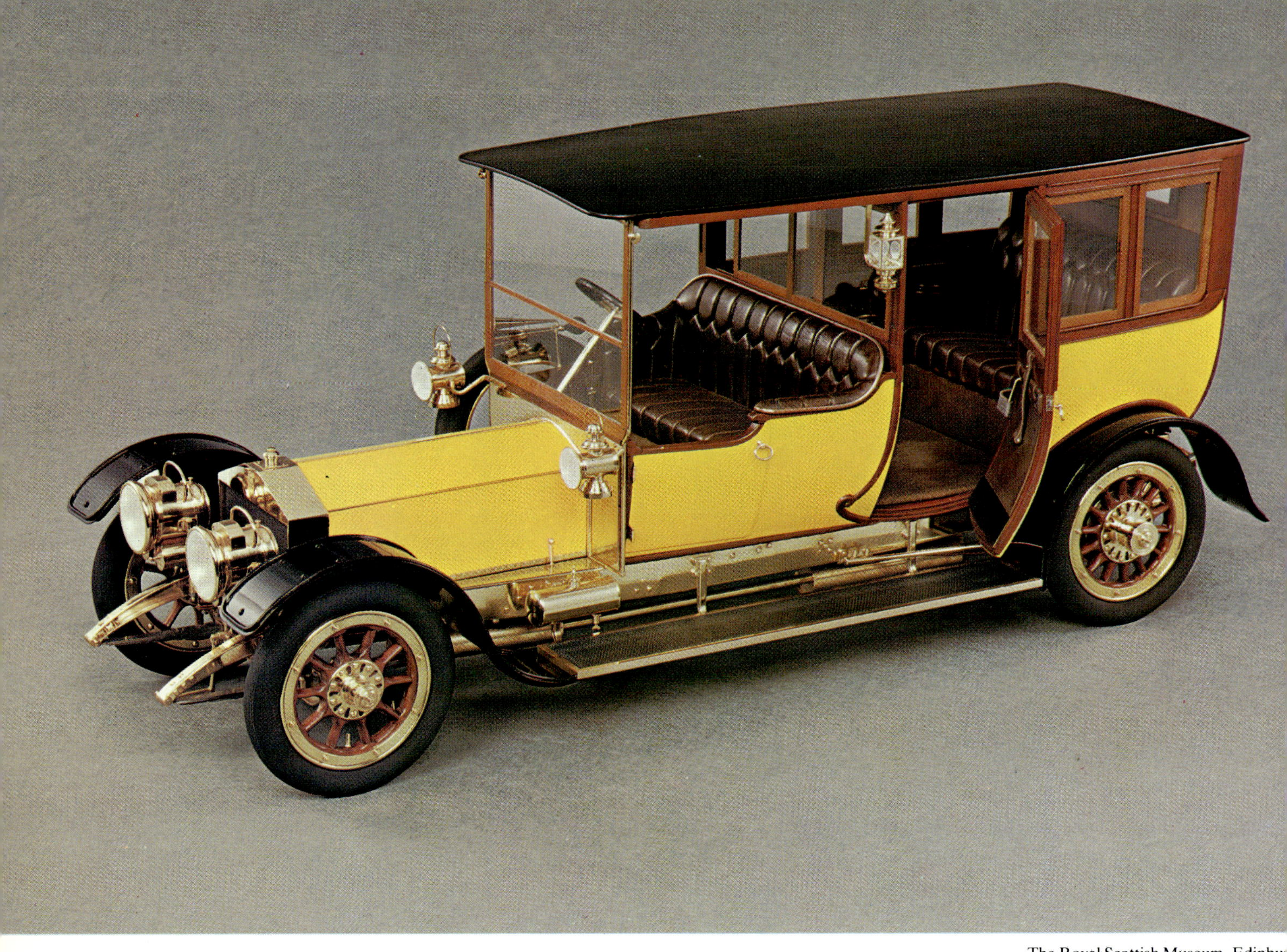

Acknowledgments

Invaluable contributions to the text of this book were provided by:
Gwen Swan, Batik Artist, Carnoustie;
Tom Gourdie, Calligrapher, Kirkcaldy;
David Heminsley, Potter, Balbirnie;
H. K. R. Whyte MBE, Embroiderer, Glasgow;
Robin Banks, Artist in Enamel, Arran;
A. D. R. Designer, Kirkcaldy;
Sax Shaw, Lecturer in Stained Glass, Edinburgh college of Art;
Alison Kinnaird, Glass Engraver, Temple;
Brian Blench, Curator of Glasgow Museum and Art Galleries, Kelvingrove, Glasgow;
Roger Millar, Head of Jewellery and Silversmithing Department, Duncan of Jordanstone College of Art, Dundee;
D. J. F. Hodge, Silversmith, Orkney;
Helen Bennett, Research Assistant (Costume and Textiles), National Museum of Antiquities of Scotland, Edinburgh;
Dr Peter Williams, Director of the Russel Collection of Harpsichords and Clavichords, Edinburgh;
James Cosgrove, Lecturer in Textile Design, Glasgow School of Art;
Donald McFall, craftsman in Wood, Arran;
Anne-Rhona Crichton, Weaver, Edinburgh;
Maureen Hodge, Tapestry Weaver, Edinburgh.

The text was edited by Sue Waterston.
With a few exceptions, the photographs for this book were produced by Paul Tomkins and A. L. Hunter of Great Stuart Street, Edinburgh.

Jack Topen
Model Rolls Royce car $\frac{1}{8}$ full size
Each model is unique with only one of each body style being made and sometimes upward of 3000 parts used in the construction.
The axles, chassis etc, are left in bright lacquered brass. Real leather is used for the seats and interiors, finest Spanish mahogany and rosewood for the wooden parts. The bodies are beaten aluminium or copper on shaped wooden frames. The completed model presented on a fine walnut or mahogany base and enclosed in a thin framed glass case.

Foreword

It is my great privilege to introduce
this publication to all those who have
an interest in the crafts in Scotland.
The book attempts to set forth in
photographs and in text where the
crafts and their finest products stand in
Scotland today.

The illustrations show the work of
craftsmen who are making a significant
contribution to the development of
their particular speciality. It is our
belief that this presentation will give
pleasure to people who love fine things.
It is also our hope that other craftsmen
and purchasers of craft objects will find
in it, inspiration and impetus to become
further involved, and particularly that
those who have the responsibility for
furbishing and decorating buildings
new or old will be moved to
commission works which will add
distinction to these buildings.

The craftsmen of Scotland and their
works are important to the life of the
people of Scotland. Beautiful
handmade objects, which also have a
sense of place, add a special dimension
to the world in which we live.
We would do well to encourage the
men and women who have decided to
devote their lives to improve their skills
at their lathes or their kilns. They are
the natural successors to and the
developers of the day-to-day
craftsmen's skills inherent in our own
people.

I should like to pay tribute to
Brigadier Paddy Doyle, my
predecessor as Chairman of the Crafts
Consultative Committee, who initiated
the concept of this book and to record
our thanks to all those who have
contributed to its preparation.

ANDREW A. HUGHES
Chairman of the Crafts Consultative
Committee.

Crafts Consultative Committee

The CCC — its history and function.

Government support for the crafts in Britain is relatively recent, beginning in 1966 when the Board of Trade made an annual grant of £10,000 to assist the development of crafts. Shared by the original Crafts Council and the British Crafts Centre in London and by the Scottish Crafts Centre in Edinburgh, the grant was continued until 1971 in the belief that well-designed crafts could make a positive contribution to Britain's exports.

A fundamental change of thinking in 1971 resulted in a transfer of responsibility for crafts development to the Department of Education and Science, bringing the crafts within the remit of the Minister for Arts. The reason for the transfer was that the primary contribution of craftsmen to the nation was, on reflection, seen to be cultural rather than economic and in furtherance of this idea, the Department made a grant to assist the formation of the Crafts Advisory Committee (CAC). The CAC's responsibility was limited to England and Wales; in Scotland, the co-ordination of crafts developed was through the Joint Crafts Committee (JCC) which was established in 1964.

The JCC was similar in membership and in purpose to the present Crafts Consultative Committee (CCC). It was serviced by the Scottish Office through the Scottish Economic Planning Department and was funded on an eighth share of the national UK crafts budget determined by the DES vote. The purpose of the JCC was to act in an advisory capacity to the Crafts Section of the Small Industries Council (SICRAS) and it was responsible for the introduction and development of many of the grant schemes adopted by the CAC and still operated throughout the UK. It was also responsible for introducing and funding the Scottish Crafts Trade Fair in 1972. With the setting up of the Scottish Development Agency in 1975, and the consequent absorption of SICRAS, the JCC was reconstituted in June 1977 as the CCC and responsibility for servicing the Committee was transferred to the Small Business Division of the Agency.

As adviser to the SDA on its crafts policy and activities, the CCC plays a major role in determining the types of assistance and support that the crafts sector in Scotland receives. Its membership, which is by invitation from the Agency, currently comprises 14 representatives from the main bodies involved with developing the crafts, art and design in Scotland, including the Design Council, Highlands and Islands Development Board, Highland Craftpoint, the Scottish Crafts Centre, the Scottish Arts Council, the Scottish Colleges of Art and practising craftsmen. The Committee which meets quarterly, is serviced by the Crafts Section of the Agency, and the Agency also provides the Committee's Assessor and Secretary.

The main purposes of the CCC are to develop new ideas and policies for furthering the interests of fine craftsmanship, in direct liaison with the organisation which will carry them through. To this end, various sub-Committies of the CCC have been established to assist the Agency's Crafts Section in the decision making processes for awards of grants and in the monitoring of crafts standards for the Trade Fair at Ingliston.

The CCC and the CAC (now the Crafts Council) exchange representation on their Committees to ensure that a balance of assistance to craftsmen throughout Great Britain is maintained and to determine areas for mutual co-operation on national crafts exhibitions and promotions. The CCC is also represented on the UK Committee of the World Crafts Council and has contributed financially to its European Secretariat.

Membership of the Crafts Consultative Committee September 1980

Andrew A. Hughes, Chairman

Tom W. Alexander
(Scottish Arts Council)

Myer Lacome, Principal
Duncan of Jordanstone College of Art

Robert Clark, Chief Executive,
The Design Council, Scottish Committee

Mrs Anne-Rhona Crichton (weaver)

Stephen Elson, Director,
Scottish Craft Centre

David Gulland (glass engraver)

Victor Margrie, Director Crafts Council

Gilian Packard (jeweller)

David Pirnie, Director,
Highland Craftpoint

Admiral David Dunbar-Nasmith,
Highlands & Islands Development Board

Sally Smith, Crafts Manager,
Small Business Division,
Scottish Development Agency

David A. Ogilvie (Assessor),
Head of Small Business Division,
Scottish Development Agency

Tom I. Geddes (Secretary),
Administration Manager,
Small Business Division

Batik

The resist dyed cloth known as batik was originally brought to Europe in the seventeenth century from the Dutch East Indies. Eventually Indonesian work declined in quality, as did most of the textile crafts in Europe, before the onset of mechanisation in the Industrial Revolution. The craft itself was practised in Europe — first in Holland, and then around 1910, elsewhere on the Continent. Its spread in Scotland in the 1920's owes much to the enthusiasm of the illustrator Jessie M. King who taught and popularised the craft. Scotland today is fortunate in having at Dundee's Duncan of Jordanstone College of Art the only textile department specialising in batik.

Working usually on silk or cotton, the artist paints a pattern with molten wax. The cloth is then soaked in dye. Where the wax has penetrated the fibres the dye will not take and when the wax is removed by ironing over paper, the wax-drawn design is left in contrast to the dyed areas. By repeating the process on the same piece up to five or six times, effects of great subtlety can be achieved. A characteristic feature of this method is the veining achieved by dye penetrating the cracks in the wax.

Because the craft does not need large, complicated equipment, it is admirably suited to small-scale, one-person workshops. There are about half a dozen people working seriously with batik in Scotland, each in their own, highly individual style. Work ranges from the one-off framed paintings of Norma Starszakowna to the silk dress-lengths made for the fashion market by Gwen Swan.

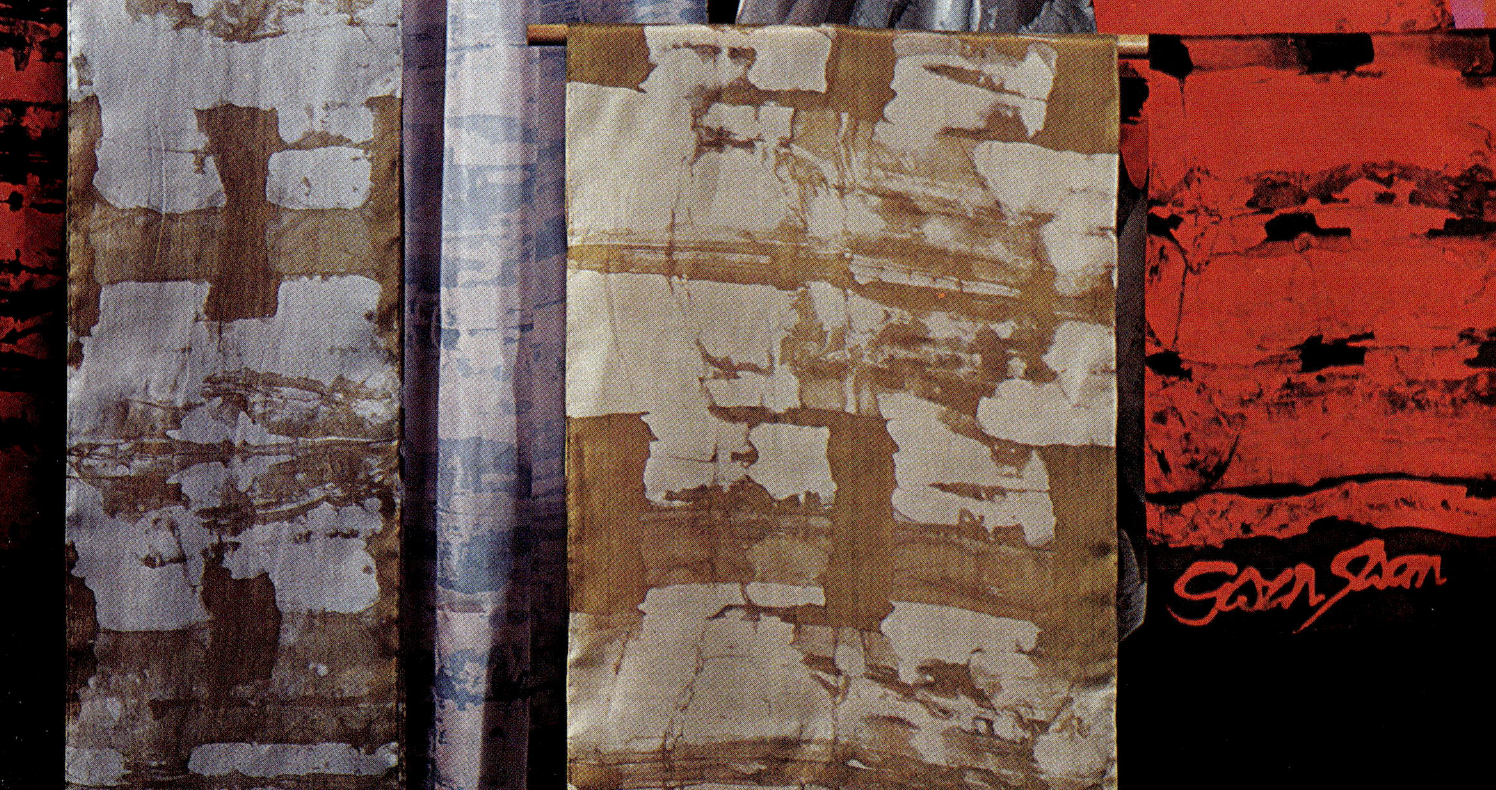

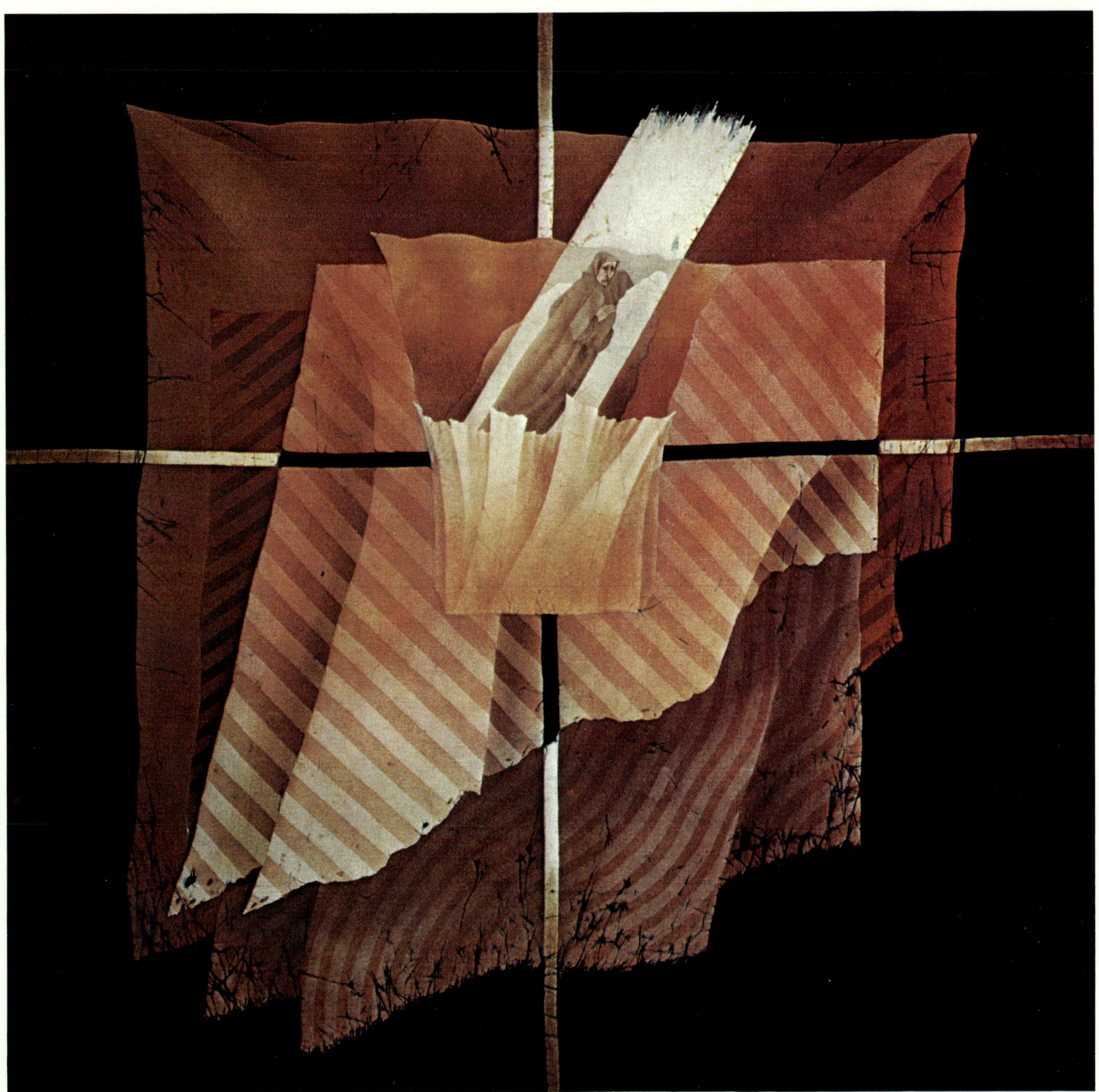

Norma Starszakowna
"Striped blanket"   68 x 68cm
Batik on silk
Norma Starszakowna explores the effects
produced by the elements of wax and dye on silk
in her batik paintings. The distinctive "crackle"
of the batik technique may be varied by the use of
paraffin wax or beeswax and small areas are
progressively waxed out until the required depth
of colour is achieved. She has always used basic
dyes, applied by fine brush, cotton wool or spray.
Some of her batiks are multi-layered pieces, in
which the surface layers are peeled back to reveal
detail below.

Gwen Swan
a selection of scarves
batik on silk, individually signed

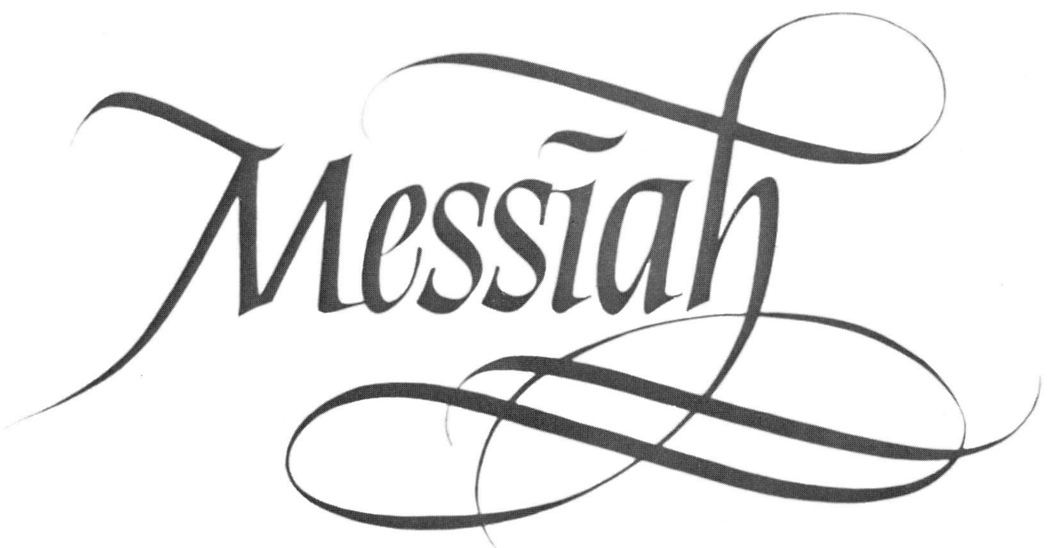

As one of the crafts which became debased during the Victorian era, but revitalised towards the turn of the century and perfected during the 1920's, calligraphy is now entering a mature but still lively phase.

Calligraphers currently practising in Scotland receive commissions from both civic and commercial sources for work as diverse as carved or drawn lettering for inscriptions; valedictory addresses; vellum scrolls; handwritten books and book jacket, greetings card and certificate designs. But the number of professional calligraphers, each working independently, is small and there is no doubt that isolation and lack of publicity tend to inhibit the number of commissions.

Unfortunately, the continuation of fine calligraphy is threatened by the fact that it has now ceased to be a diploma or degree subject in Scottish colleges of art with the exception of Glasgow School of Art. Here George Thomson lectures and also specialises in computer letter design and lettering for reproduction, carrying on the teaching tradition of Irene Wellington and Nora Paterson, whose former students at Edinburgh have been successful in becoming members of the London-based Society of Scribes and Illuminators.

Some of the better known calligraphers in Scotland today are Stuart Barrie, Head of Graphic Design at Edinburgh College of Art and a specialist in lettering for reproduction; Andrew Chisholm, whose main work is in typography and sign systems; David Lang and Michael Ashley, two young calligraphers who teach evening classes at Edinburgh and freelance as designers of certificates; John O. R. Martin who has his own graphic design studio in Edinburgh and caters for calligraphy, illustration and typography and George L. Thomson of Fife who specialises in the Roman capital in drawn, painted and carved form and has developed a modern Uncial suitable for his Gaelic broadsheets. Both George L. Thomson and Tom Gourdie, M.B.E., who also lives in Fife, have published books on calligraphy and the teaching of handwriting. The Simple Modern Hand, an Italic, has been developed by Tom Gourdie and widely adopted as a style for primary schools. Donald Murray of Aberdeen concentrates on the Uncial and Half-Uncial, and Joan Tebbutt, a former teacher at Glasgow, now provides lettering and tooled decoration to books for the Douglas Cockerell Bindery at Grantchester. Both she and Avril Gibb of Skelmorlie carry out commission work as does H. J. Blackman, who since his retirement as a Ceremonial Artist to the Greater London Council, has continued to specialise in copper-plate inscriptions.

It may be that greater recognition of the calligraphers in Scotland will stimulate commissions and professional recognition. There is a growing concern to establish a Scottish Calligraphic Society and to mount more regular exhibitions of work.

George L. Thomson
"Scribe"
Calligraphy for the cover of "Scribe, a scribe's notebook" published by Canongate Publishing Ltd of Edinburgh 1978.
42×32 cm

3 *Calligraphy*

George Thomson
"Messiah"
The lettering was designed as part of a poster for Dunblane Cathedral Arts Guild. The letterform is derived from a pen-executed italic but has been modified considerably from that script. Gouache on line board.

Beryl Tittensor
"The shepherd's Kitchen"
Old Scots saying written in a rounded italic hand with a turkey quill on goat-skin vellum using hand-ground stick ink.
19·8×13·8 cm

Stuart Barrie
"A brave man dies but once, a coward dies many times"
In the last ten years Stuart Barrie has concentrated on drawn and painted panels of lettering similar to the example shown.
25×18 cm

From the eighteenth century numerous Scottish factories, particularly in the Glasgow area and at Prestonpans and Portobello near Edinburgh produced a wide range of ceramics, both decorative and domestic. This tradition of handmade pottery continues with renewed vigour today, though many of its proponents are art school graduates rather than craft trained as in the past. Behind much of this renewal in what is by far the most popular modern craft lies a search for alternative life styles unconnected with the normal channels of industry and commerce. There is a quiet but decided attempt by many people to find other ways of being; or as Sir Gordon Russell has said, at 'finding a quality of life in place of a standard of living'.

Expression of these attitudes is contained in a self-sufficient approach to workshop economy: home-made kilns fired with waste oil or wood, clays and glazes prepared from local materials such as ash or granite dust, construction of equipment from scrap material. Increasingly these practices make economic sense even on a small scale.

From the public viewpoint too there is a continued search for wares individually made and this demand is met in the hundreds of craft shops throughout Scotland, in exhibitions by individuals or groups of potters, and of course in the craftsman's own showroom. Even in remote areas potters are sought out by visitors anxious not only to buy, but to see how pots are made. The wheel continues to be a magnetic draw for spectators. Purchase of special pieces made to order is quite common as is direct selling by the potter to visitors. The dialogue between customer and craftsman is one of the attractions for both parties.

Individual attitudes to potting are reflected in the size and organisation of the workshop. Some are quite small one-man studios, while others may consist of a small group of two to four people working with a master potter. Size however does not reflect the resulting excellence or otherwise. Indeed many of the finest producers may work in a part-time capacity supported by teaching, thus leaving themselves free from market pressures to create individual work.

Likewise technique varies enormously but throwing on the wheel surely constitutes the central discipline for most craft potters. The texture, plasticity and firing qualities of the clay body interact with the spirit of the potter and the form he creates — full bodied, rough or smooth, taut or relaxed — the variations are endless and are evident in the ribbing of the final fired pot, whether it be on an intricate form or on the humblest vessel.

However, many other methods of making are also used by potters: coiling or slab building, direct modelling, press moulding, jigger and jolleying and slip casting. Sometimes a potter may use several methods on one piece.

Surface decoration is an aspect of ceramics which only a few years ago was not often seen in studio pottery — form being kept simple and uncomplicated by pattern. Recent trends have seen a revival of many aspects of decoration using a wide range of imagery — landscapes, floral designs, abstract and figurative subjects, all executed in many different materials and techniques — slips, oxides, underglazes, enamels or lustres and applied by brushwork, inlay, slip trailing, graffito or spraying.

Glazes compounded from natural minerals fused at varying temperatures give shiny, lustrous, matt or dry surfaces which interact with the clay bodies. Of the many clay bodies used by potters from rough toasty coloured to smooth grey or white, a type of ware increasingly used is porcelain. A technically demanding material it needs precision in execution but once this is conquered the resulting pristine whiteness lends itself to intricate and delicate decoration.

The range of the modern Scottish potter is well covered in these pages. Much of the work illustrated is highly individualistic, often not meant for use but to be regarded as an aesthetic object in its own right.

In contrast to these works are those potters, numerically the largest single group, who primarily make functional pots. Domestic ware is a demanding field. It requires quality bodies, even throwing and turning, and consideration for such things as snugly fitting lids, good pouring spouts, well balanced handles. Quality production is required for a wholesale market which requires constant vigilance in these matters where purchasers use the pots daily. It is sad to say that many practitioners underestimate the requirements of good domestic potting. However the examples shown here demonstrate fluency in throwing, turning and handling which lend the pots a pleasing vitality in execution and design.

The potters and ceramists represented here are a cross-section of a hundred or so professional potters working in Scotland. While many other examples could have been shown, both the informed observer and the layman can see what is possible in this very popular craft.

4 *Ceramics*

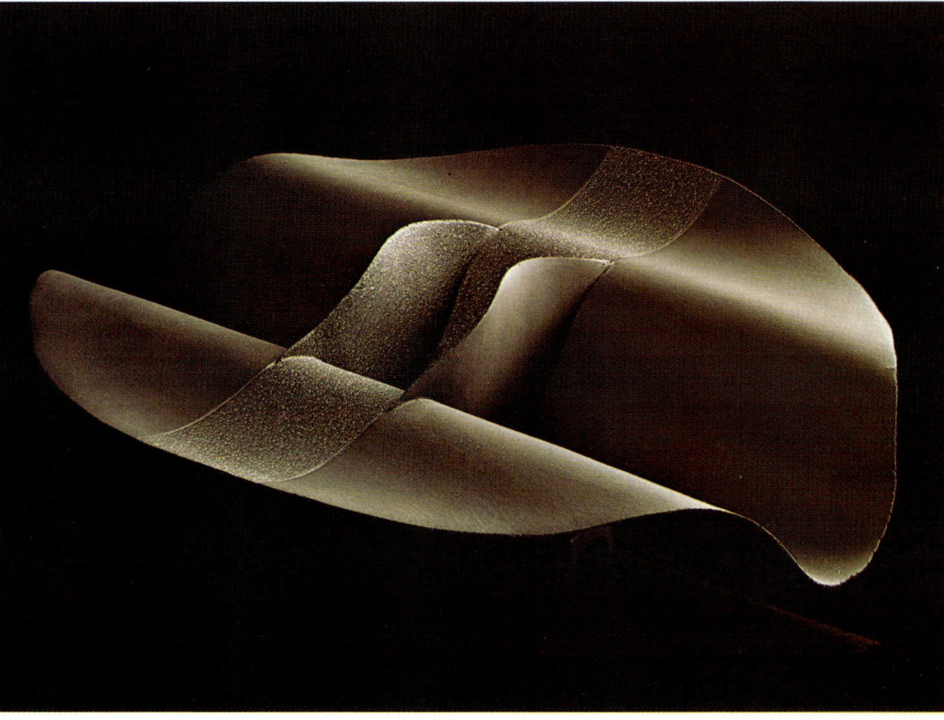

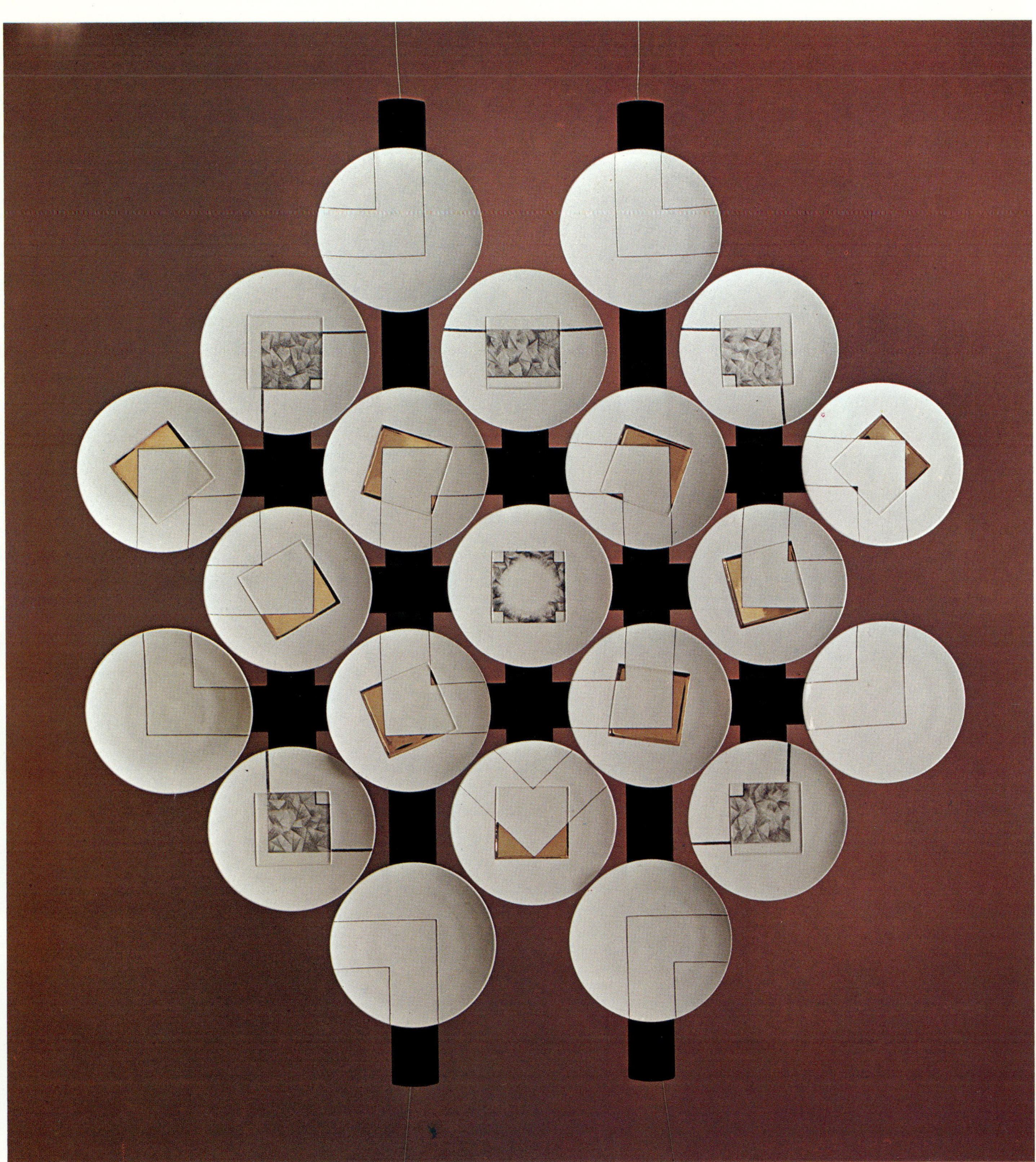

Tony Franks
"White clouds like a belt encircle the mountain's waist"
Ceramic construction in black basalt clay.
Sandblasted texture.
Fired to vitrify at 1160°C.

Dave Cohen
Plate composition
The development of the plate composition began three years ago and consisted of hand-thrown plates. In contrast the present plates are made from the jigger using the basic industrial technique. The jiggering method was necessary to enable geometric shapes to be accurately reproduced from the same form so that each plate would line up precisely with the adjacent plate. Because of the accuracy of duplication and the quantity of plates used in this composition the development of a wooden grid on which to hang the plates added a further design element.
Each plate was high fired to 1260°C and sprayed with a white slip, after being bisqued. Ceramic pencil and 1060°C commercial glaze was used after this high firing and lustre gold was fired over the commercial glaze to a temperature of 750°C.

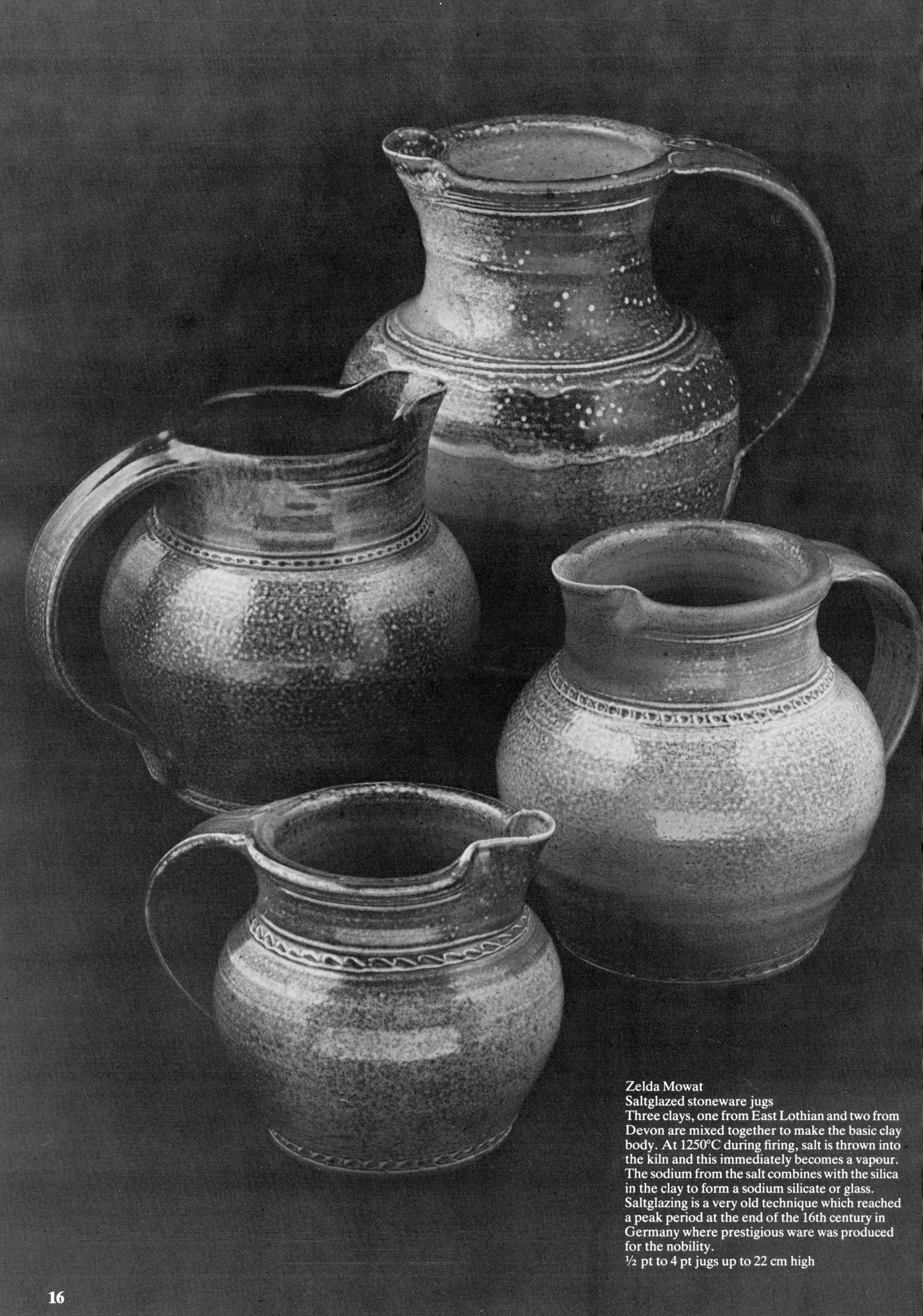

Zelda Mowat
Saltglazed stoneware jugs
Three clays, one from East Lothian and two from
Devon are mixed together to make the basic clay
body. At 1250°C during firing, salt is thrown into
the kiln and this immediately becomes a vapour.
The sodium from the salt combines with the silica
in the clay to form a sodium silicate or glass.
Saltglazing is a very old technique which reached
a peak period at the end of the 16th century in
Germany where prestigious ware was produced
for the nobility.
½ pt to 4 pt jugs up to 22 cm high

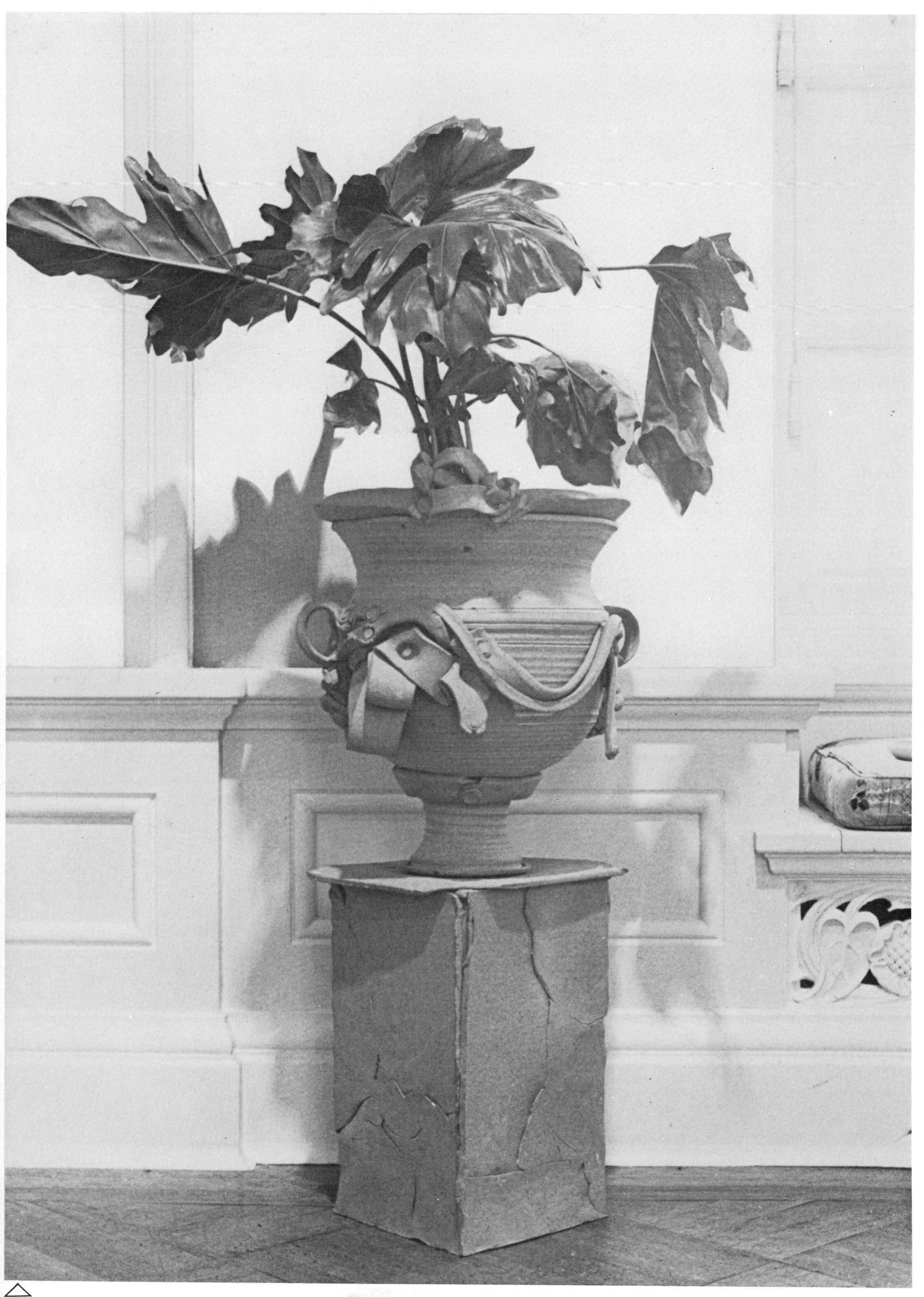

Douglas Davies
Stoneware planter
Unglazed stoneware planter fired to 1280°C in gas-fire reduction kiln. The main bowl and the small stand are thrown, the base being hand built in a wooden mould. The main bowl has holes in the base to allow for drainage and all three sections are joined together. The swashes and elaborate clay decoration are added at the leather stage and great care is required in drying.

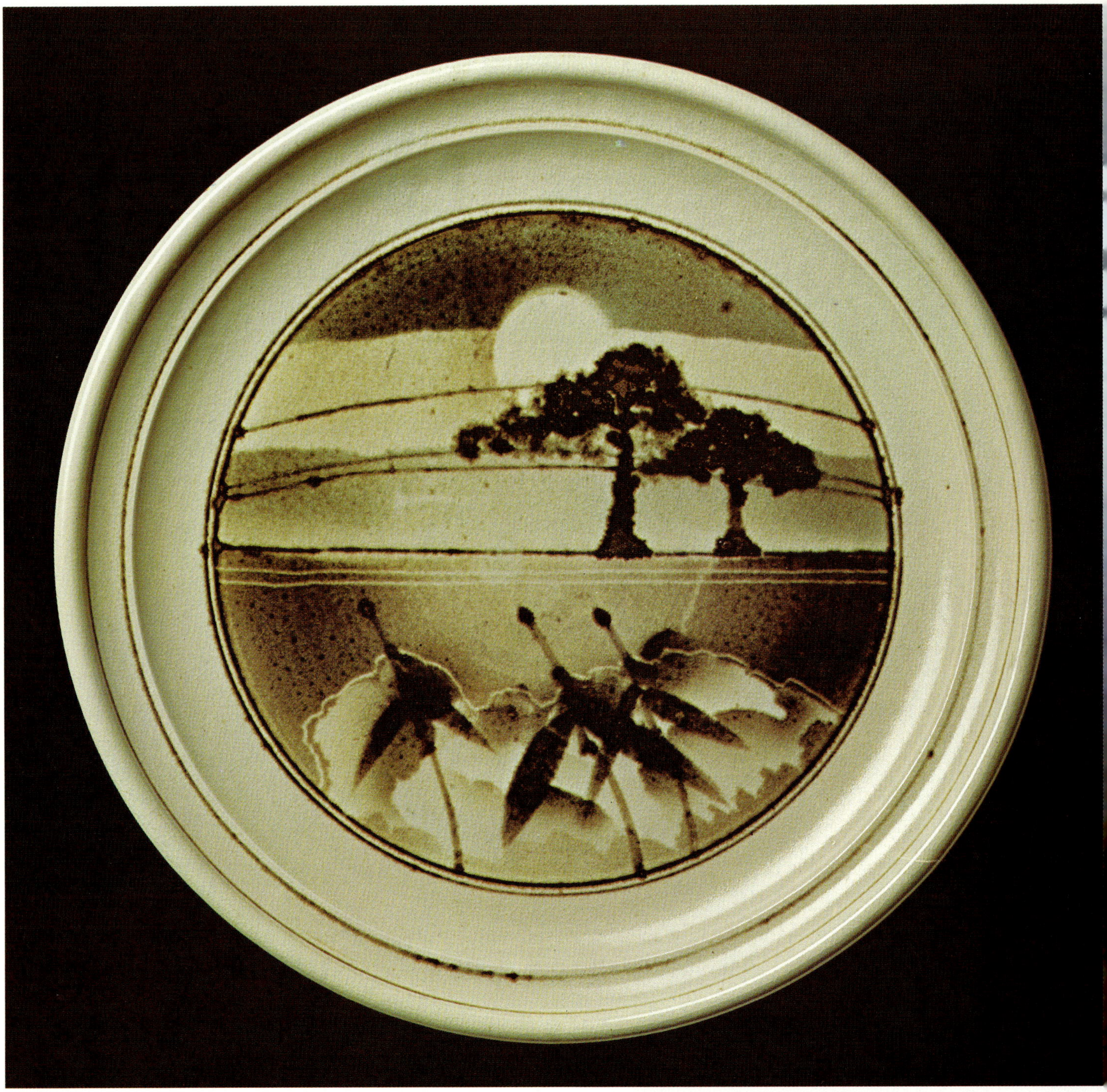

Ian Pirie
Porcelain plate with painted decoration

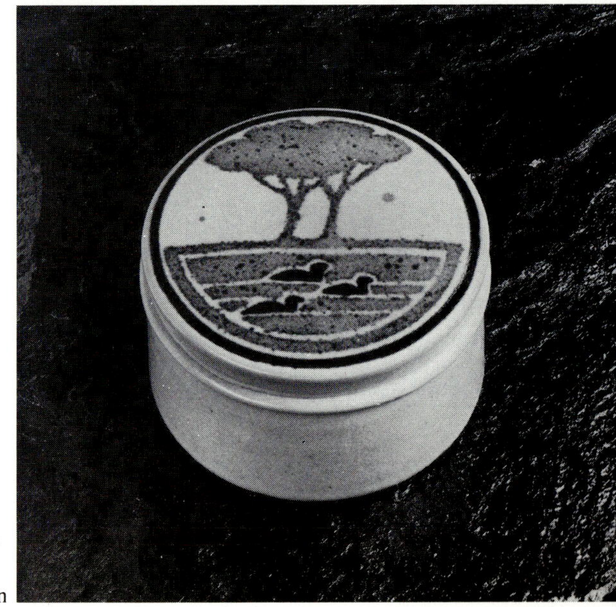

Bill Brown
Porcelain box with resist decoration

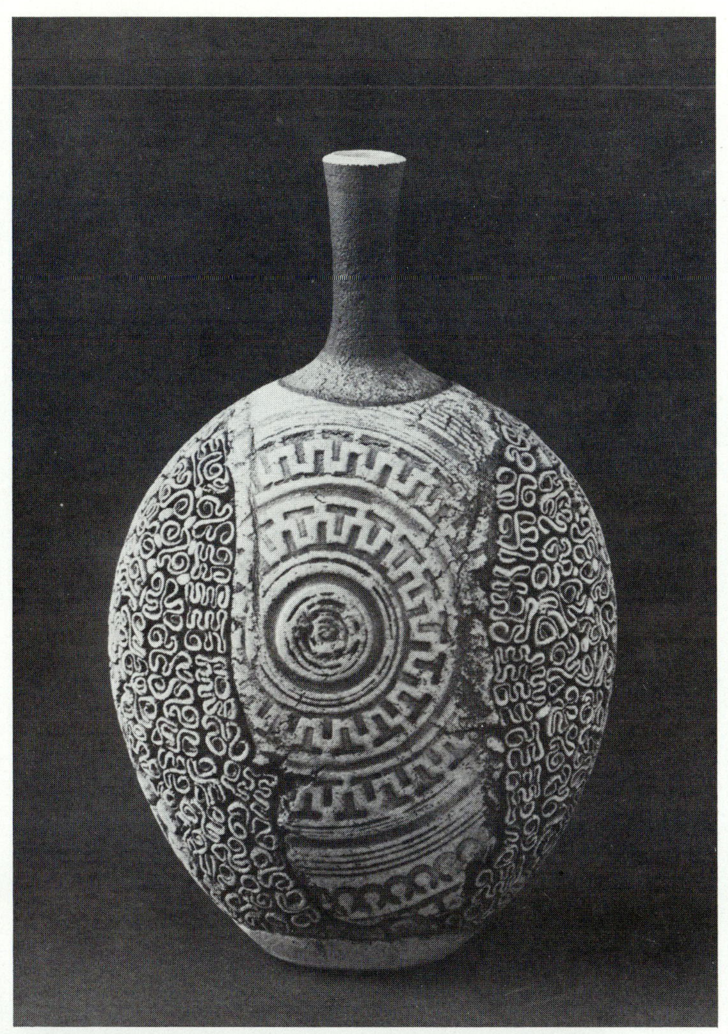

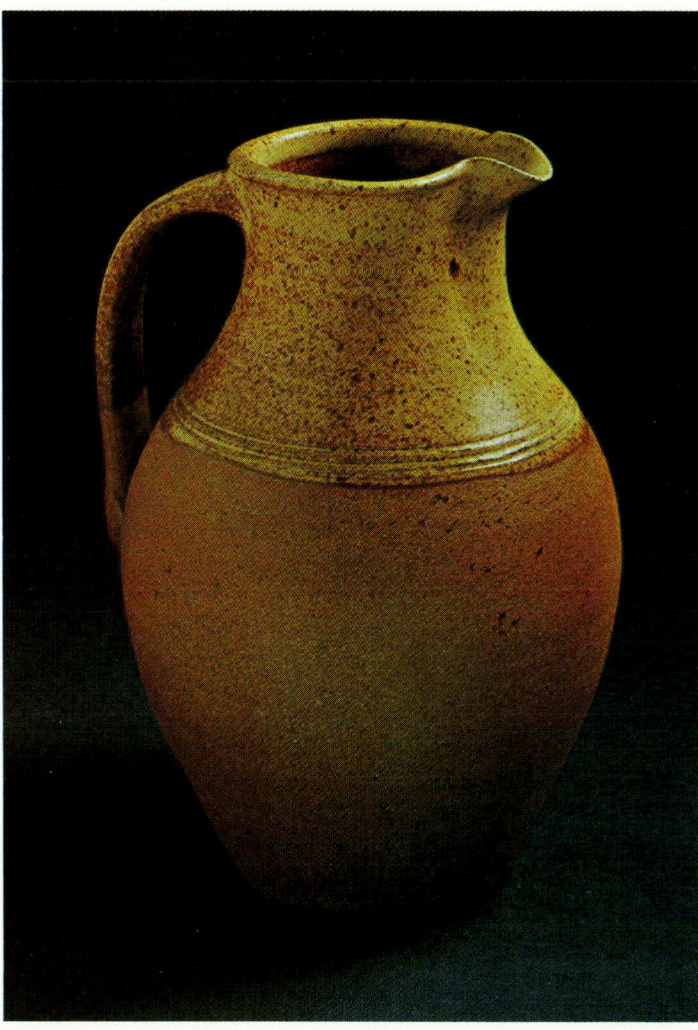

Joe Finch △
Jug
Hand thrown pot, once-fired in a large wood-fired kiln to a temperature of 1300°C.
24×17 cm

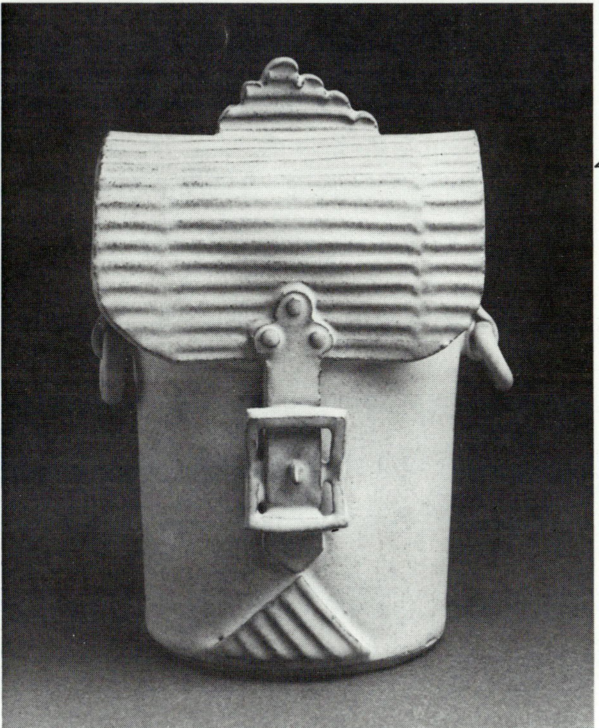

△Bill McNamara
Handbuilt pot in plaster mould with surface texture built into the pot in coils and slabs. Fired in a reducing atmosphere and coloured with washes of red iron oxide and black manganese oxide.
22 high. ×13×80 cm

Stewart Johnston
Grey stoneware bag with impressed decoration
In addition to his domestic and decorative stoneware, Stewart makes non-functional objects. The piece illustrated is one of a number of every-day objects.
The piece is first bisque fired and then all decoration and glazing completed before firing to 1260°C in either oxidising or reducing atmosphere. The clay body is St Thomas's and virtually all objects start life on the potter's wheel.
16·5×13 cm

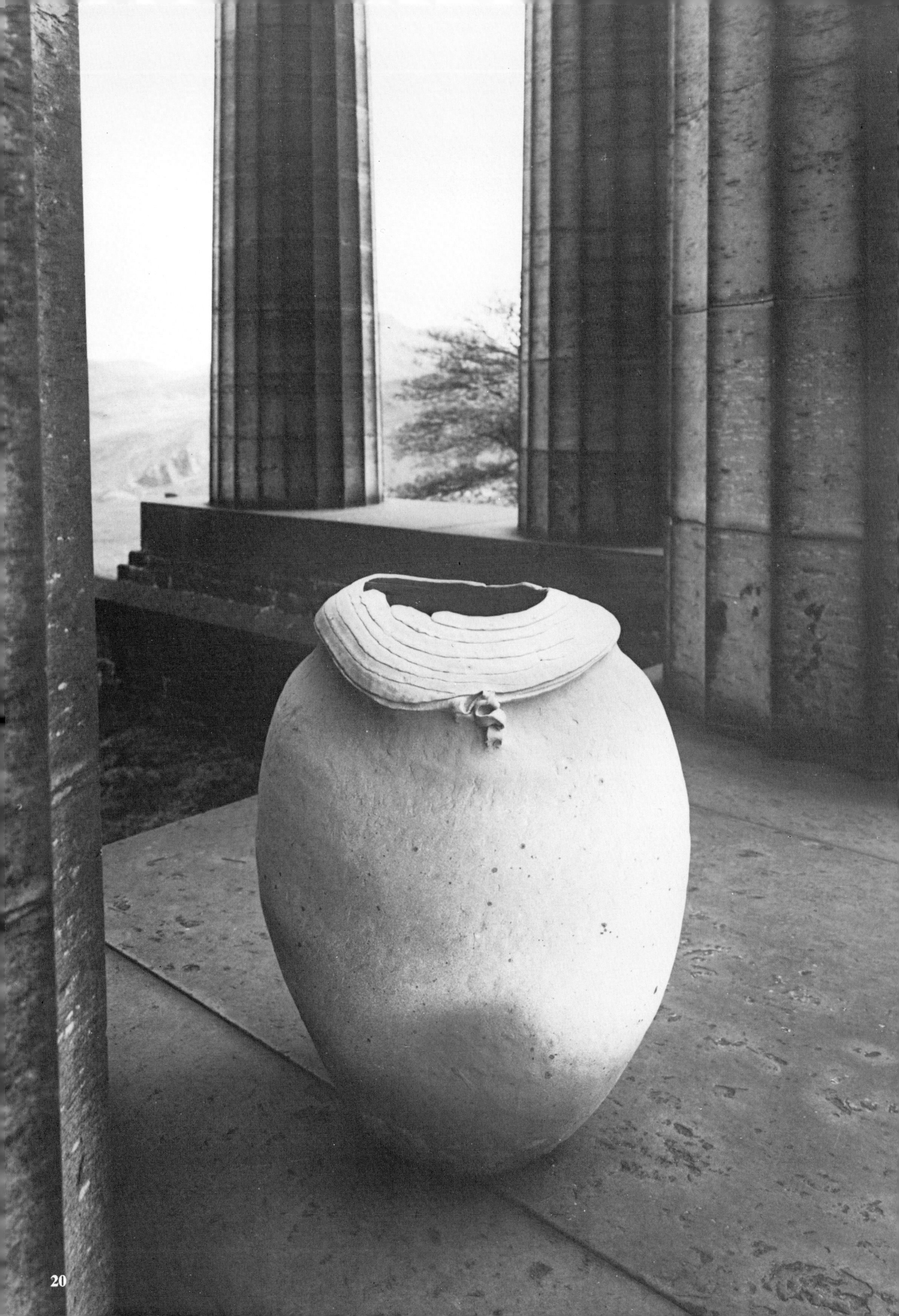

Iain Nelson
Large Urn
Handbuilt, decorated with several layers of
sprayed slip. Reduction fired stoneware (1230°C)

Susan Senior
''Black piece with white seeds''
The base of this piece is of stoneware clay built up
in the slab technique coloured by iron and
manganese oxide (no glaze) and fired to 1280°C
in a reduction firing. The white seeds are handbuilt porcelain fired to 1280°C and secured by
cotton thread. The seeds are also unglazed to
retain the white quality of the clay.
28×16 cm

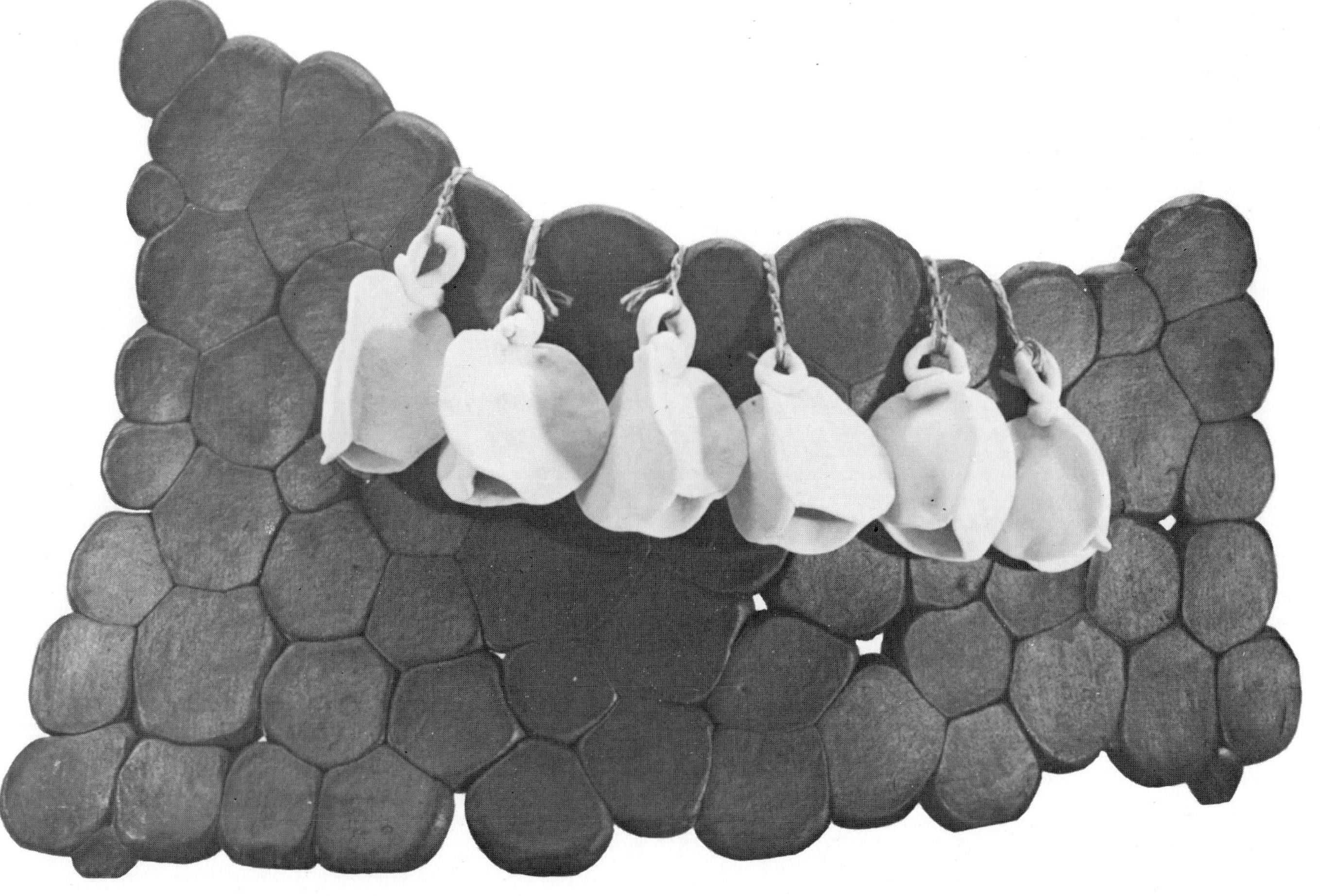

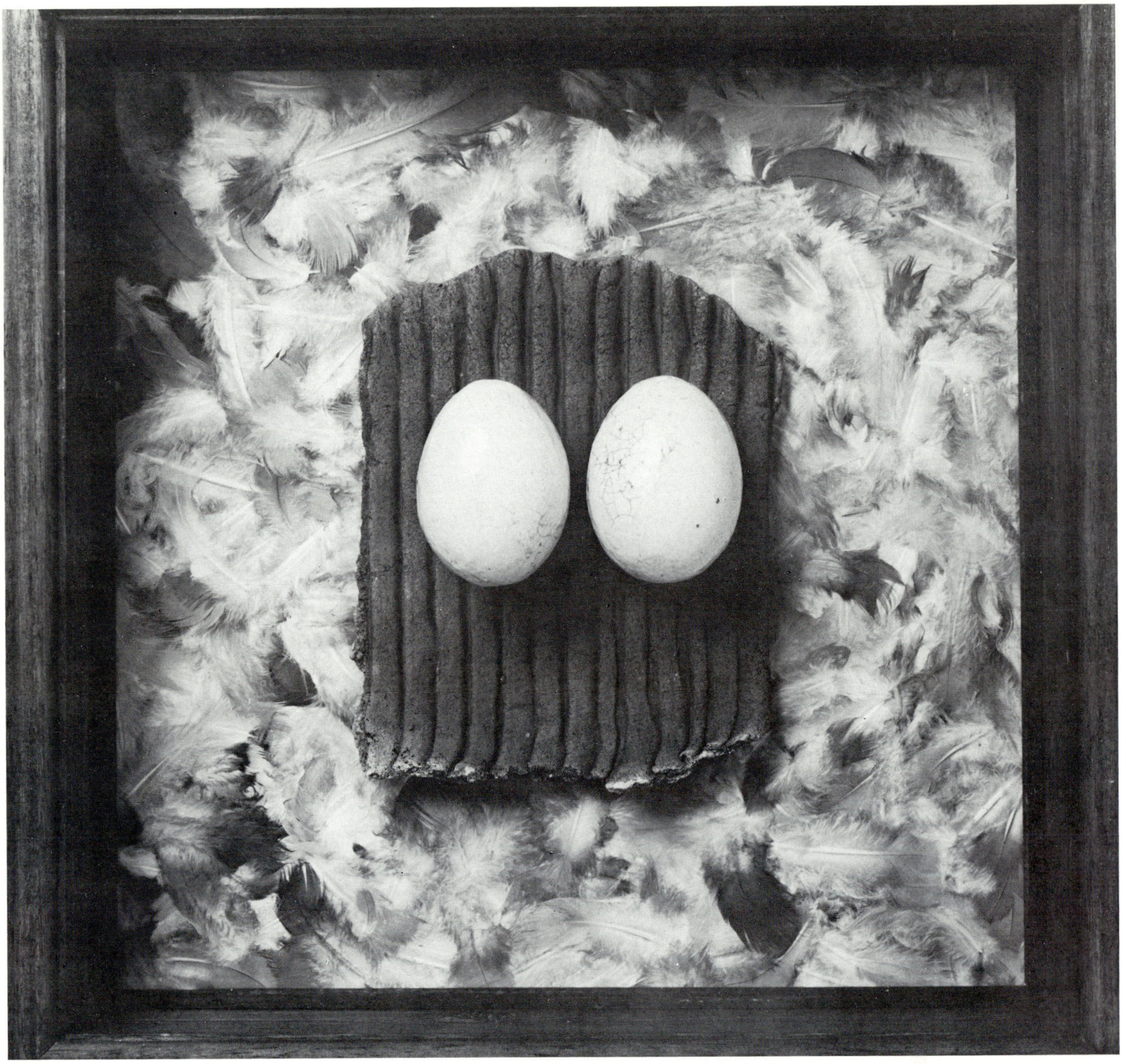

△

John Cumming
"Phoenix box No 1"
This is the first in a series of ceramic sculptures on
the same theme. The box is backed with wood
pigeon feathers. The raku ware in the box is
glazed with a soft alkaline glaze, heavily reduced
in sawdust after firing to 950°C in a paraffin-
fuelled dustbin kiln.
34×34 cm

Margery Clinton
Slip cast pottery glazed in iridescent lustre.
The technique of lustre glazing, which originated
in the Middle East, has always been a hazardous
one, notoriously difficult to control, with the
secrets of the process being closely guarded. It
involves a period of reduction in the kiln at a
critical temperature, but the finished object has a
rich colour and a highly reflective surface.

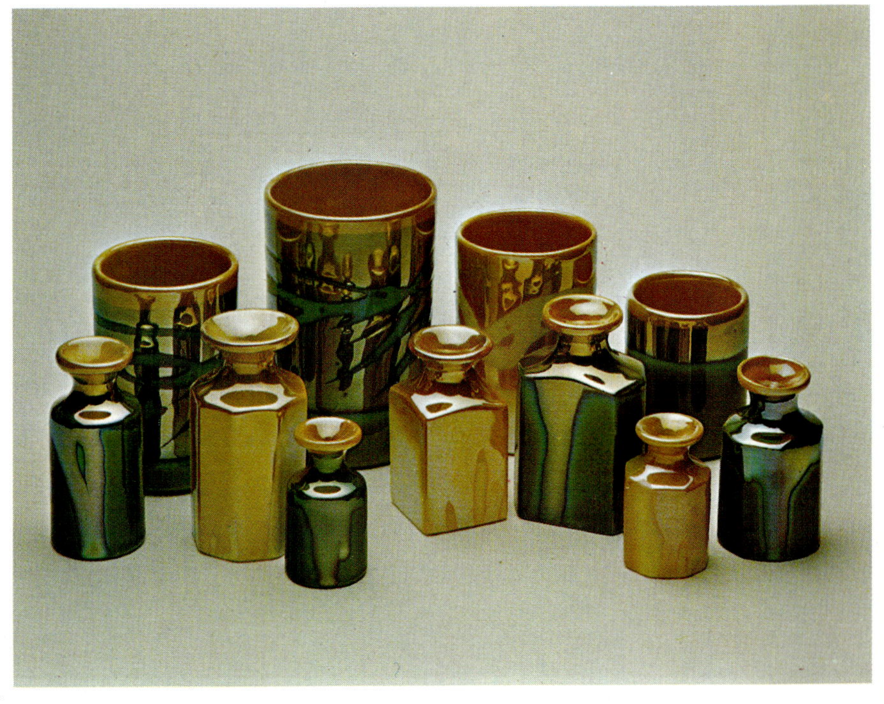

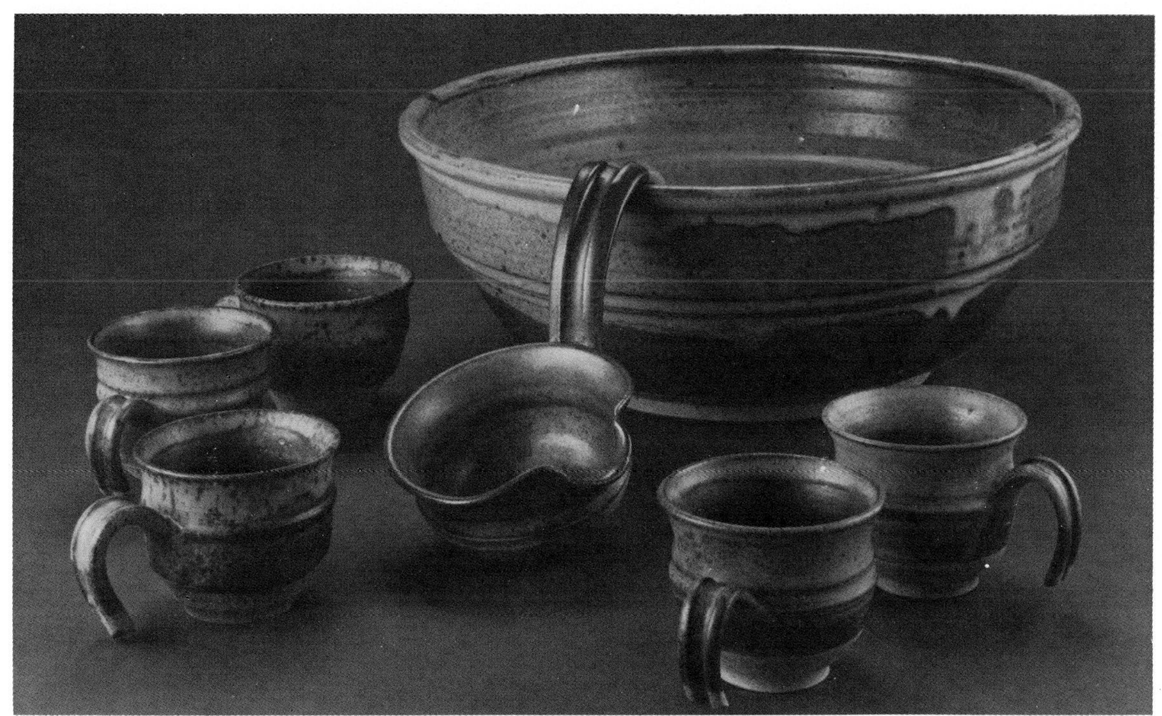

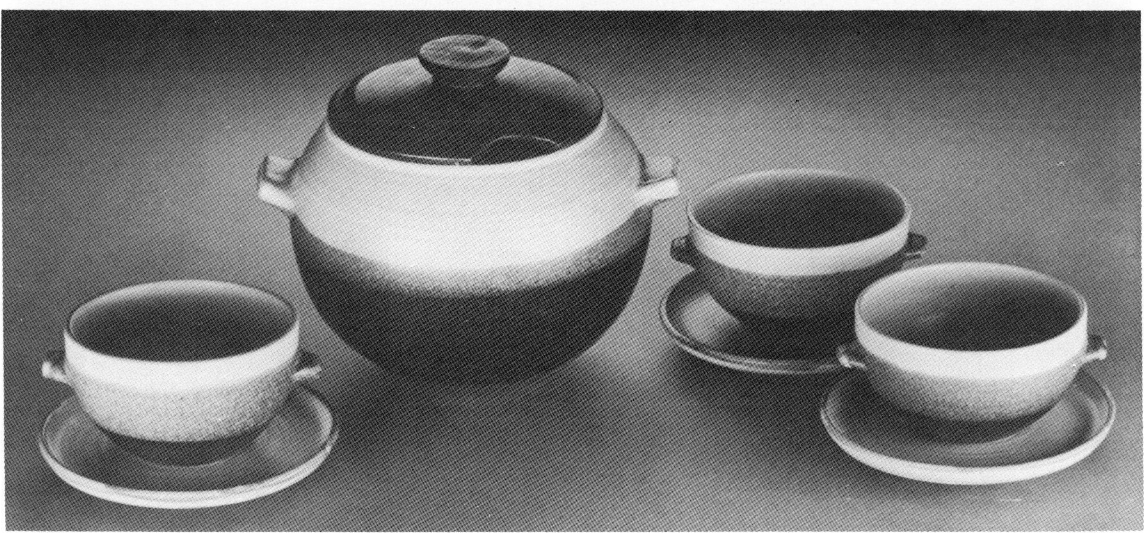

◁ Janet Adams
Punch bowl set in reduced stoneware with a
wood-ash glaze.
30 cm diameter.

◁ Gretl Shapiro
Tureen and bowls
Hand thrown stoneware, fired to 1280°C. Glazed
in brown and white.

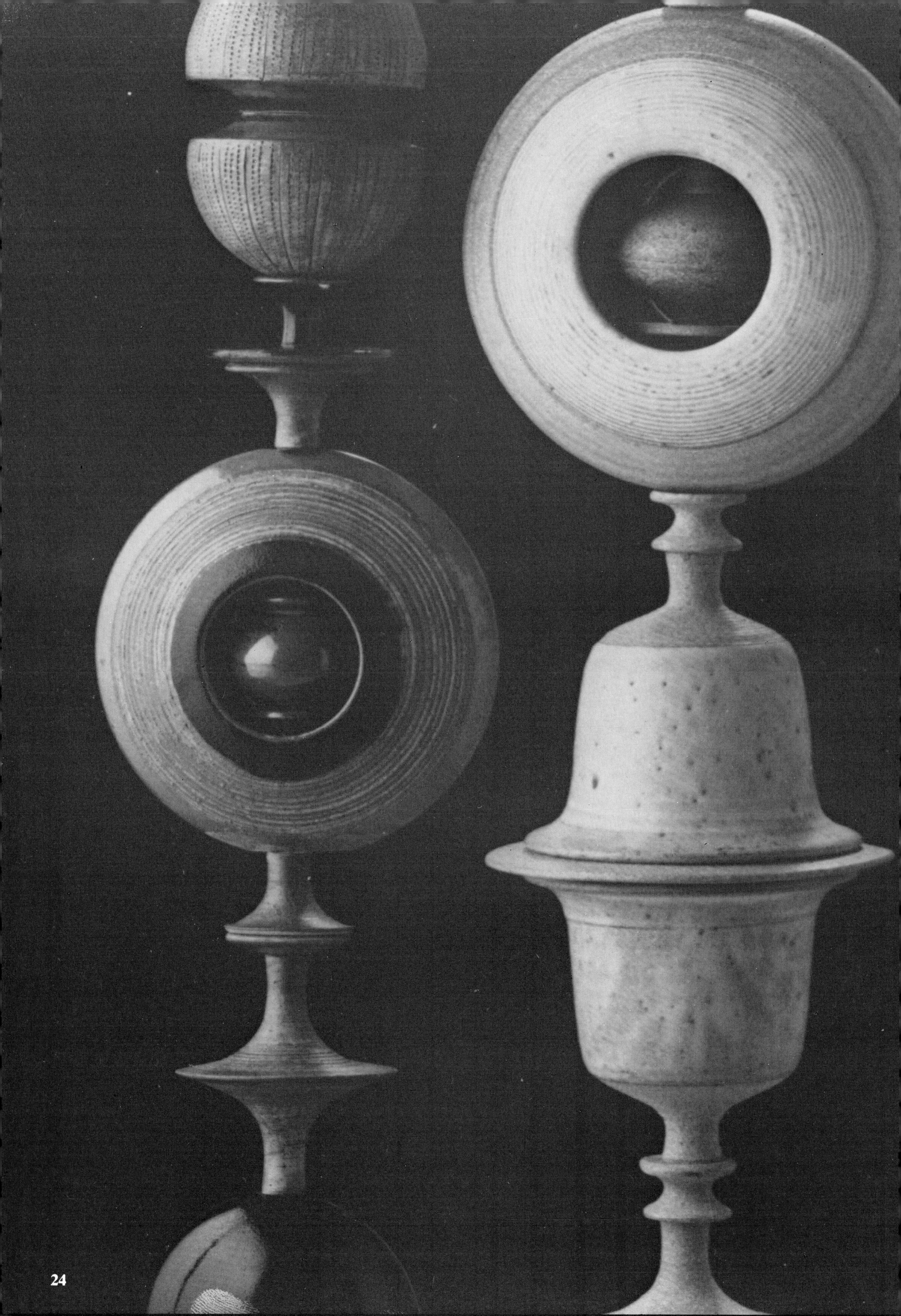

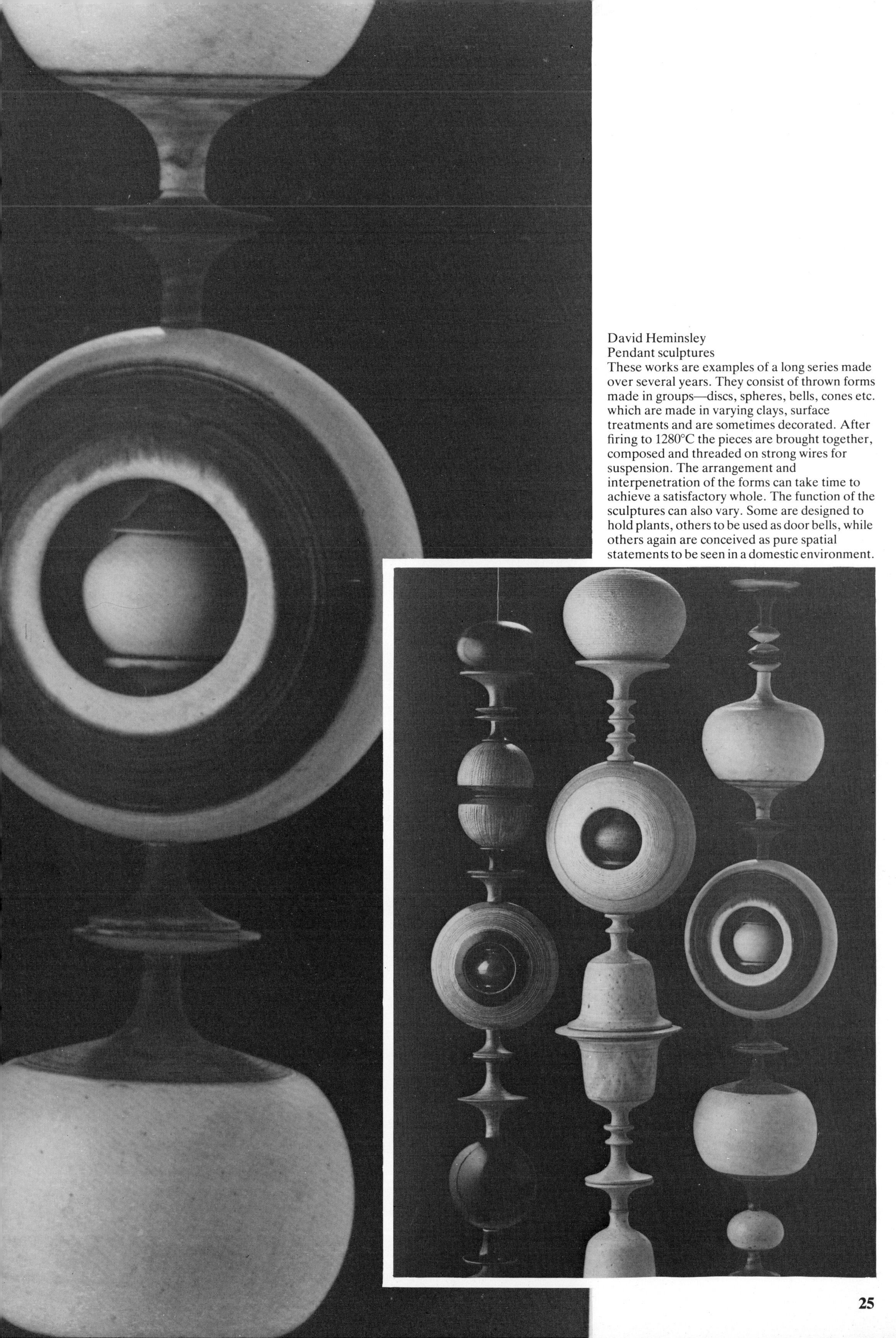

David Heminsley
Pendant sculptures
These works are examples of a long series made
over several years. They consist of thrown forms
made in groups—discs, spheres, bells, cones etc.
which are made in varying clays, surface
treatments and are sometimes decorated. After
firing to 1280°C the pieces are brought together,
composed and threaded on strong wires for
suspension. The arrangement and
interpenetration of the forms can take time to
achieve a satisfactory whole. The function of the
sculptures can also vary. Some are designed to
hold plants, others to be used as door bells, while
others again are conceived as pure spatial
statements to be seen in a domestic environment.

5 *Embroidery*

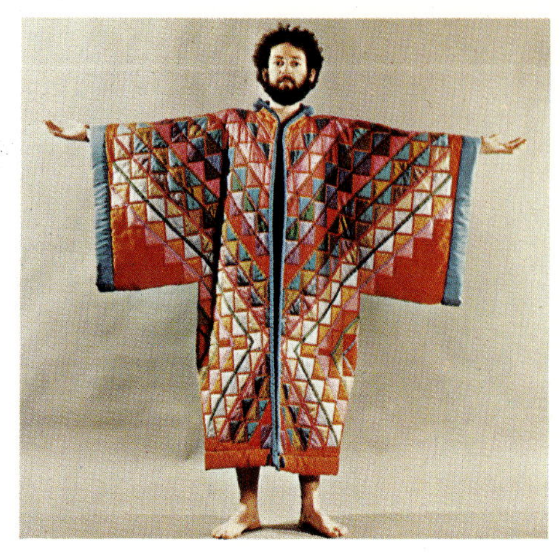

Embroidery, an extremely versatile art, spans the centuries mirroring each age and reflecting the social history of all countries. Interesting and very beautiful examples survive from the past to give evidence of skills and techniques which provide a rich heritage for the modern embroiderer — church vestments, rich garments and domestic furnishings.

Scotland was fortunate in that an entirely new approach to embroidery was evolved at the Glasgow School of Art in the 1890's. This Art Nouveau revival was to lay the foundation for the embroidery of our own time, with teachers such as Jessie Newbery and Ann Macbeth. Carried forward still on the enthusiasm and abilities of talented teachers, it has become an adaptable art form, admirably suited to the climate of research and experiment which currently prevails. Established techniques are no longer regarded as sacrosanct but rather as starting points for personal experiment.
The enormous range of materials available entice the student to create fabrics which are the raw material of abstract structures, and to induce threads to behave in quite new ways.

Colour is a vital element in embroidery, and materials with varying textures and light reflecting qualities provide the embroiderer with a complete palette.

Contemporary embroiderers produce panels, hangings and other wall decorations as well as three-dimensional objects. Often, no single technique predominates in a piece which becomes an amalgamation of several skills, particularly in church work where the need to portray symbolic forms calls for ingenious methods. Church commissions may include a pulpit fall or a cloth for a Communion table, or a hanging or screen for the chancel area or vestibule. Public buildings can similarly be enhanced by embroidery but commissions have been very few. By contrast in Scandinavia a proportion of the costs of any new building is set aside to purchase a work of art.

What of the future? There is in embroidery an intrinsic excellence quite independent of period. This need not be incompatible with an adventurous spirit for the future, but it represents a challenge.

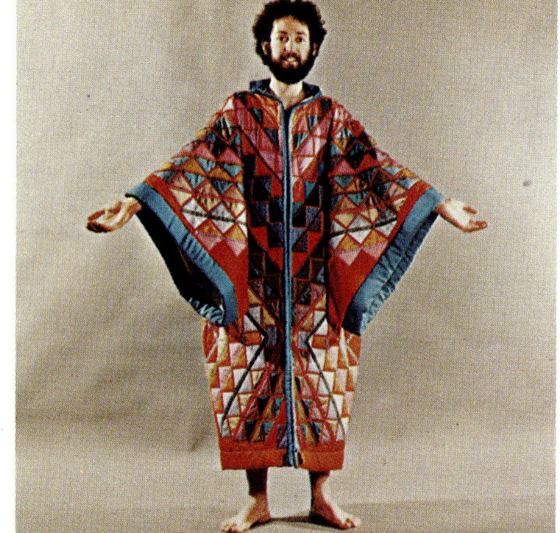

Crissie White
"Joseph's Coat of Many Colours"
Designed and embroidered for the Department of Surgical Neurology, Dundee Royal Infirmary. The coat is hand embroidered on a silk background, specially woven by Dalgleish of Selkirk. The applied patches are almost all of wild silk from India or Thialand. 25 yds of fabric have been used altogether.

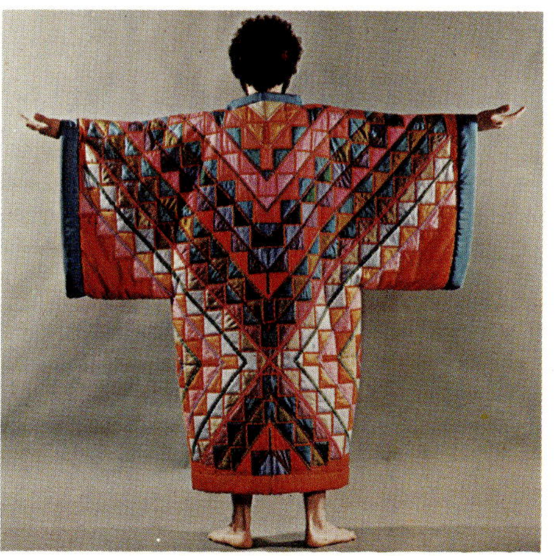

Hannah Frew Paterson
Embroidered panel "Sea and Sand"
The brief for this commissioned hanging contained the wish that the patron's interest and love of seascape should be contained in the finished work. This element was resolved during the initial stages of design by analysing the movement of waves and the relationship between sea and sand. The overall result depended completely on three-dimensional methods of working and the design divided into four distinct sections of different character.
175×68 cm

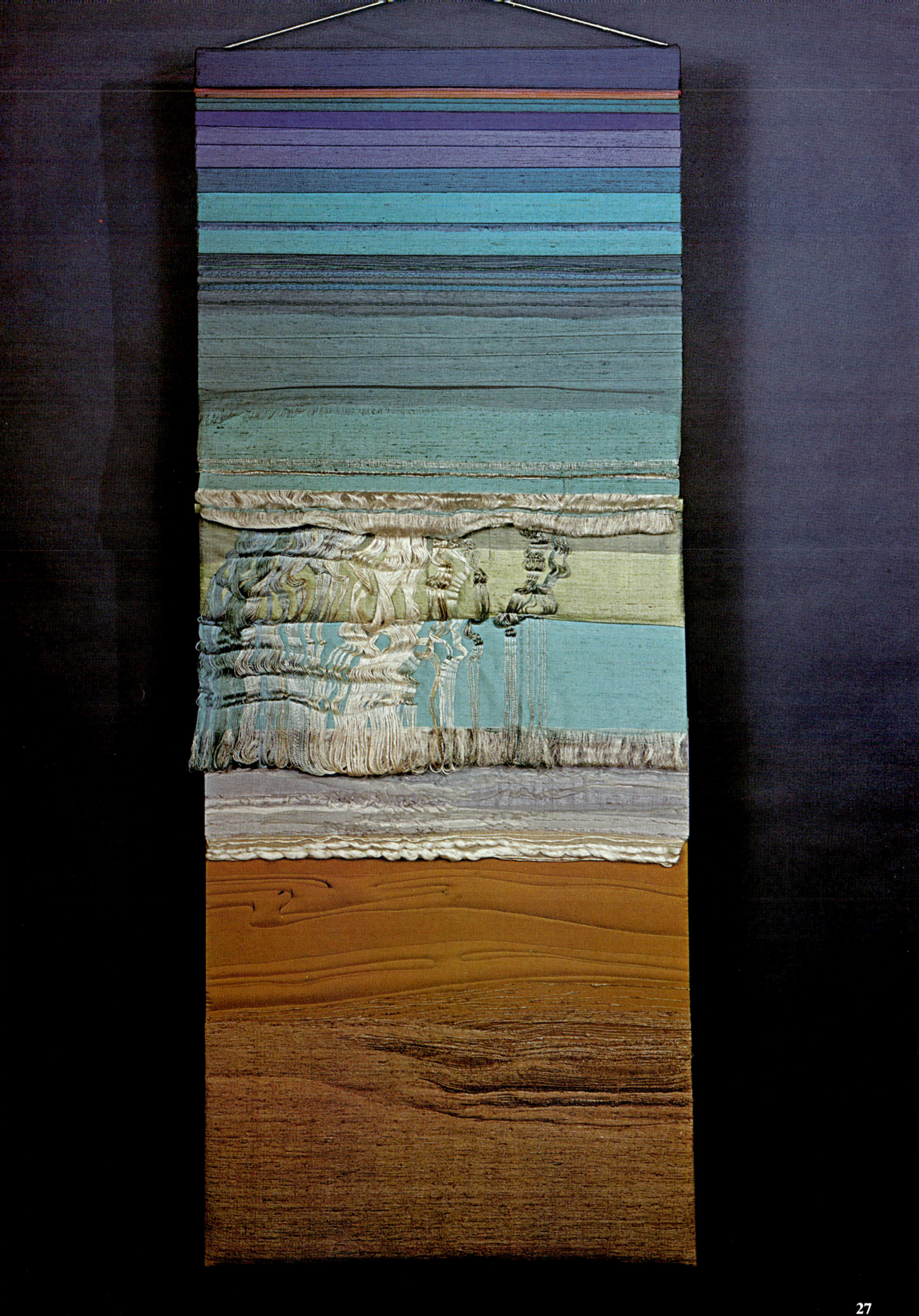

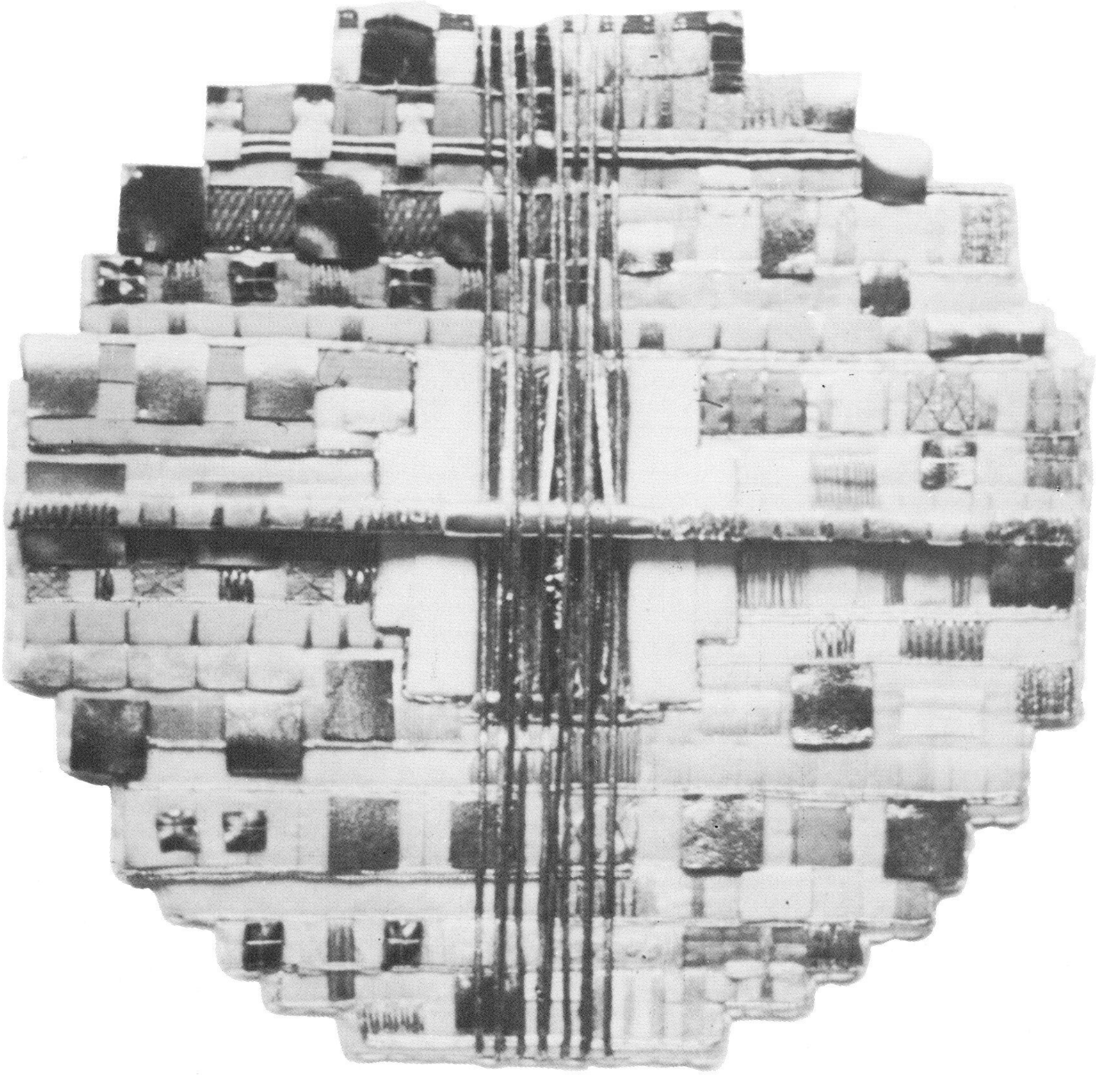

Kathleen Whyte
White pulpit fall for St Brendons Church—Bute
On a background of white silk the design is a variation on the familiar Cross/Circle theme. The circle is built of horizontal ridges held in place by various methods including blocks of gold and silver kid. In a circular movement, lone, pale silvers turn into dark golds—"The darkness and the light".

Mary Johnstone
Gold embroidered chess set
The chess pieces are made from soft kid in gold and dark blue embroidered in various stitches with different types of gold threads (ie Japanese gold, pearl purls, purls, bullion, plate gold and sequins). They are stuffed with foam rubber.
The board is linen, embroidered with drawn-thread lines and a pulled stitch decoration on the squares—the linen is mounted over a sheet of gold plastic.
55×55 cm   largest piece 7·5 cm high

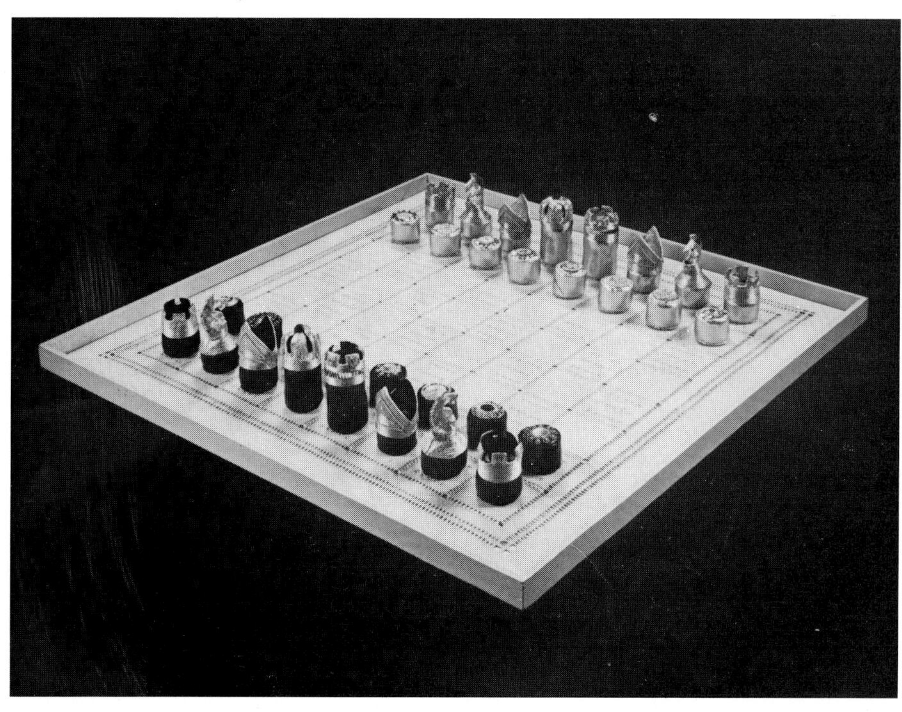

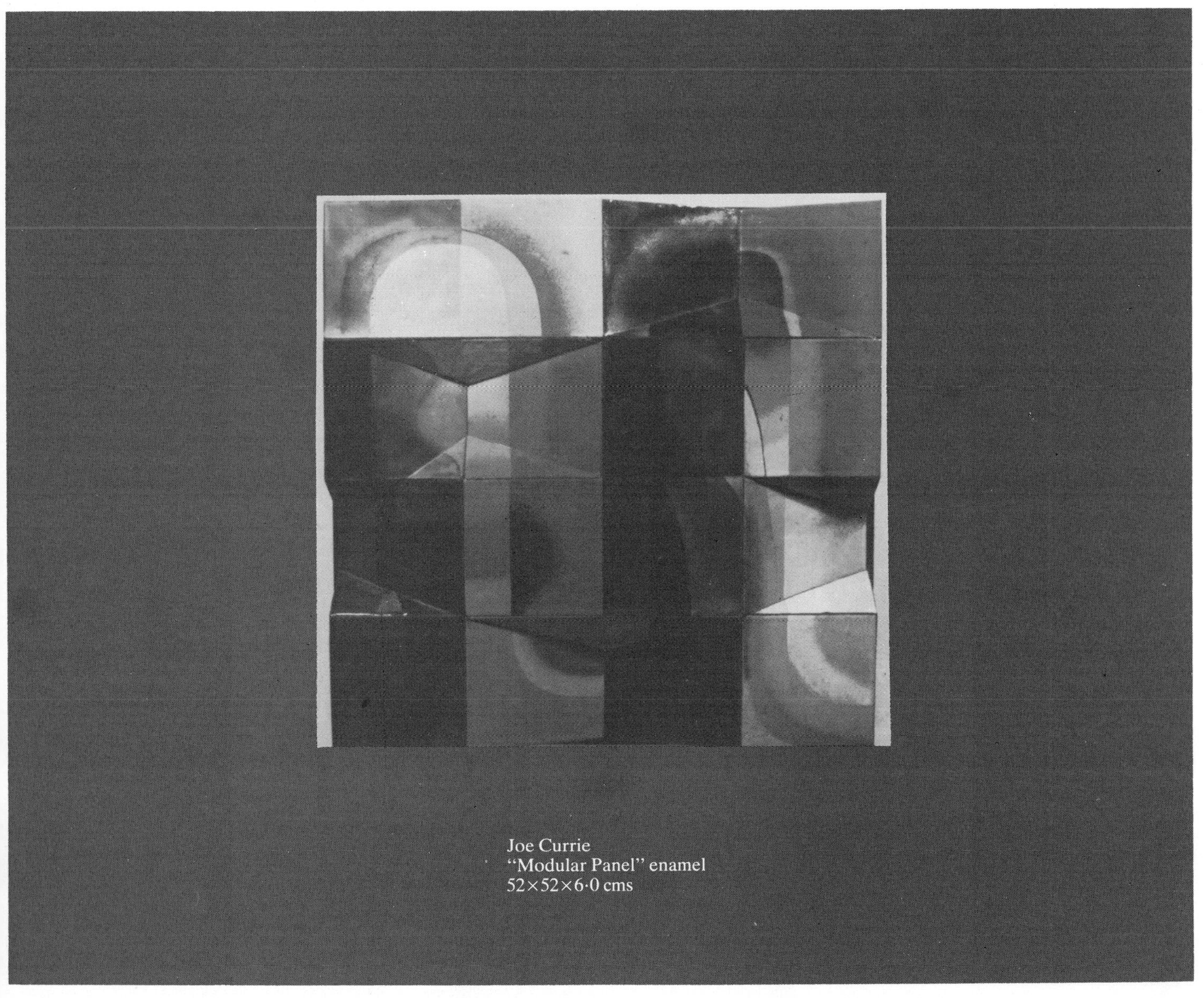

Joe Currie
"Modular Panel" enamel
52×52×6·0 cms

6 Enamel

Fire and water are the two essential elements in enamelling, other than the actual materials: a source of heat for fusing the glazes to metal, and water for washing the enamel glaze to a fine clear colour. The natural water of the West of Scotland, with its acid quality is entirely suitable for this purpose. Whether you grind the colour to powder yourself, from the broken lumps of glass in a mortar, as jewellers do, or buy already powdered enamel for larger-scale work, the preparation of the glazes is also done under running water. Robin Banks is lucky to have her own supply, from a hill straight into the studio. There has also been co-operation from the Hydro-Electric Board to provide a supply for a very large furnace; all this has helped her to set up perfect conditions for the production of enamelled dishes and large panels.

It must be said that there is no such thing as 'cold enamelling', a term which has become as prevalent as 'enamel paint' used to be. Enamel by definition in every European language means a fusion of glass to metal by heat, and has no more to do with the use of resin, than fibreglass and resin have to do with bronze-casting.

There are certain problems in enamelling in Scotland: firstly it is extremely expensive. The rapid firing which produces good results needs a great deal of power — a high kilowattage for an electric furnace.

Also as the traditional centre of glazemaking in this country is the Midlands, very heavy parcels of glaze have to be sent to the far corners of Scotland, from Stoke-on-Trent, at ever increasing postage and haulage rates. The same applies to sheet copper, although that is more generally available over the country and there are suppliers in Scotland. A greater problem is the isolation in which country enamellers have to work. It is a constant mental exertion to fight for perfection, no less, with rare opportunities for comparison, discussion or encouragement compensated only by ideal physical conditions of work.

Furniture

The country which produced — and rejected — the innovative furniture designer Charles Rennie Mackintosh at the turn of the century still tends to demand old and tried design. But however skillfully made, spinning wheels and reproduction furniture do not advance the craft. For Scottish furniture to have a future, the makers must be prepared to be progressive both in method and design, to have originality of conception as well as excellence of execution.

The designer craftsman needs to have sympathy with his materials, an understanding of the construction methods to be used and a kinship with the machinery and tools employed. Clarity in the initial design, the presentation drawings and communication with the client are also vital factors.

Among the present generation working in Scottish furniture is a nucleus of craftsmen, many of them trained as designers in schools of art, who share these and similar pre-occupations. Two groups who trained with the innovative English maker John Makepeace, but chose to work in Scotland, are Hans Elleflaadt and the members of Adelstrop Woodworks. Elleflaadt also trained in the furniture industry, and has a healthy disdain for those who go through arduous manoeuvres by hand when a machine can do the job just as effectively. Kenneth Anderson, whose work is illustrated on these pages, has developed an angular style, often using the technique of inlaying to produce integral landscape decoration on his furniture. In contrast, Tim Stead creates imposing pieces of furniture in

which the character of the wood is allowed to predominate, and as in the Cafe Gandolfo in Glasgow, he enjoys treating the furnishing of an interior as a piece of integrated design.

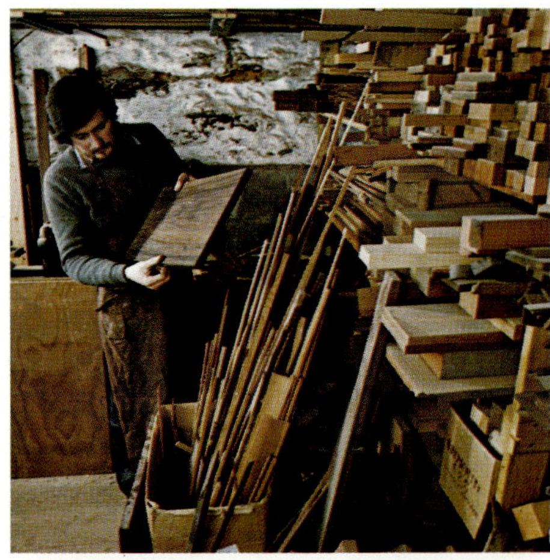

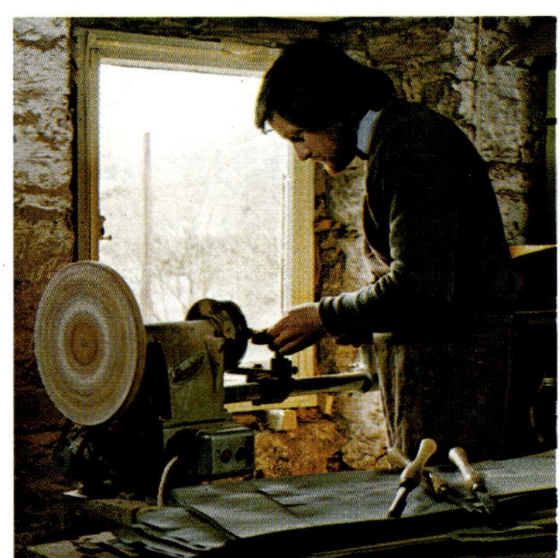

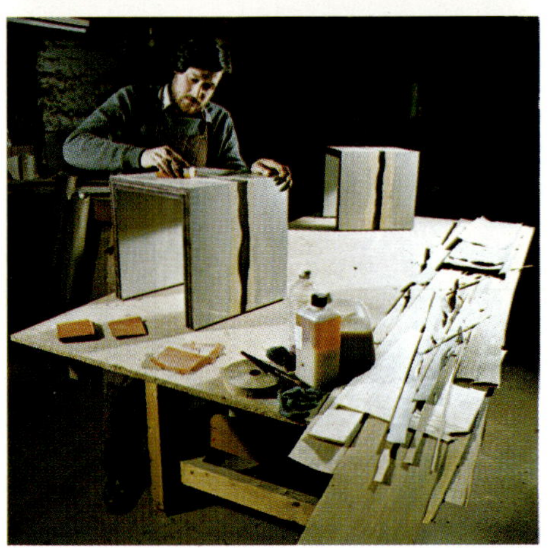

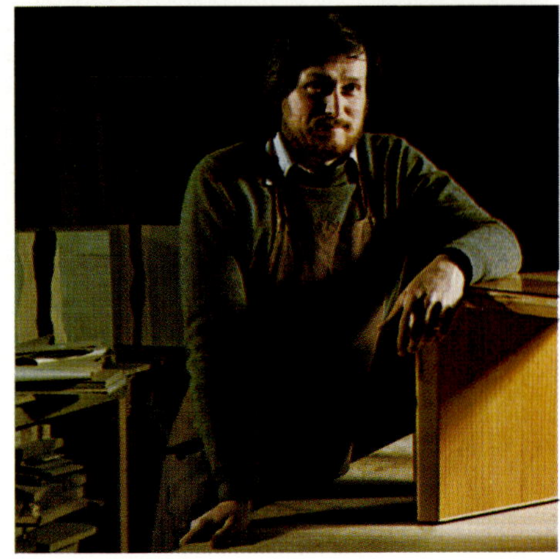

Kenneth Anderson
Kenneth Anderson in his workshop at Braco. Inlaid chest of drawers and table shown at the house of the owner

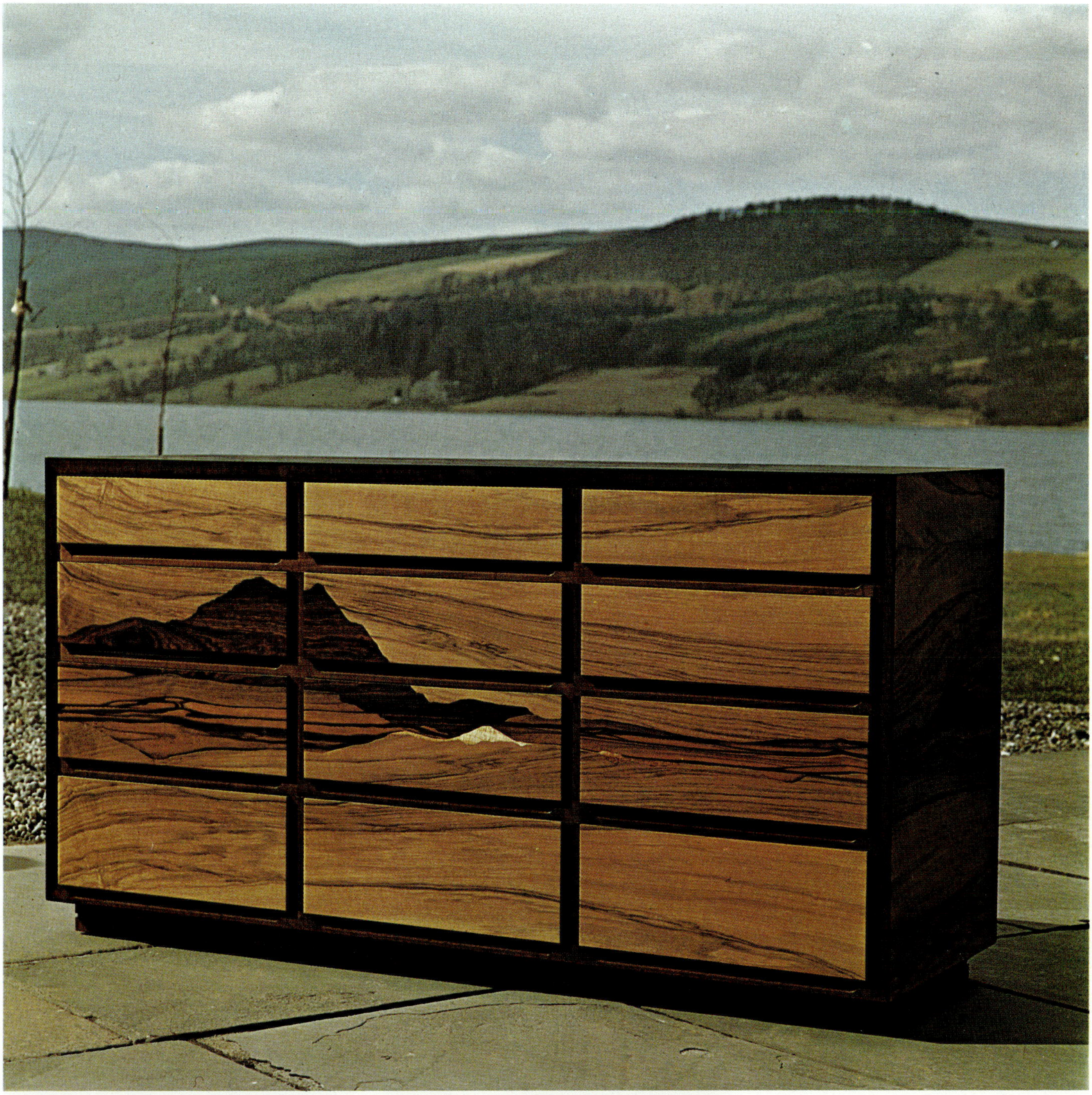

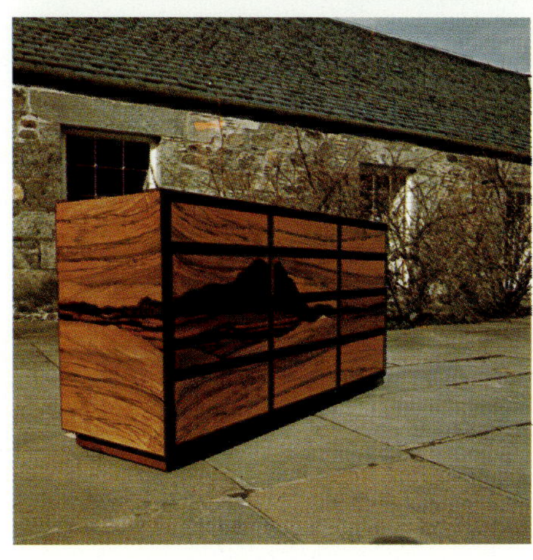

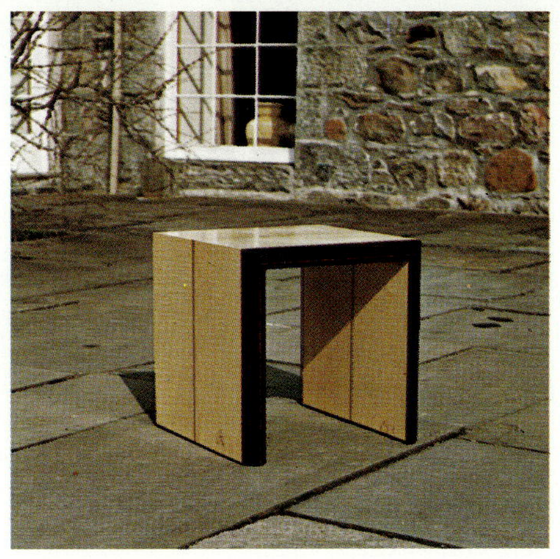

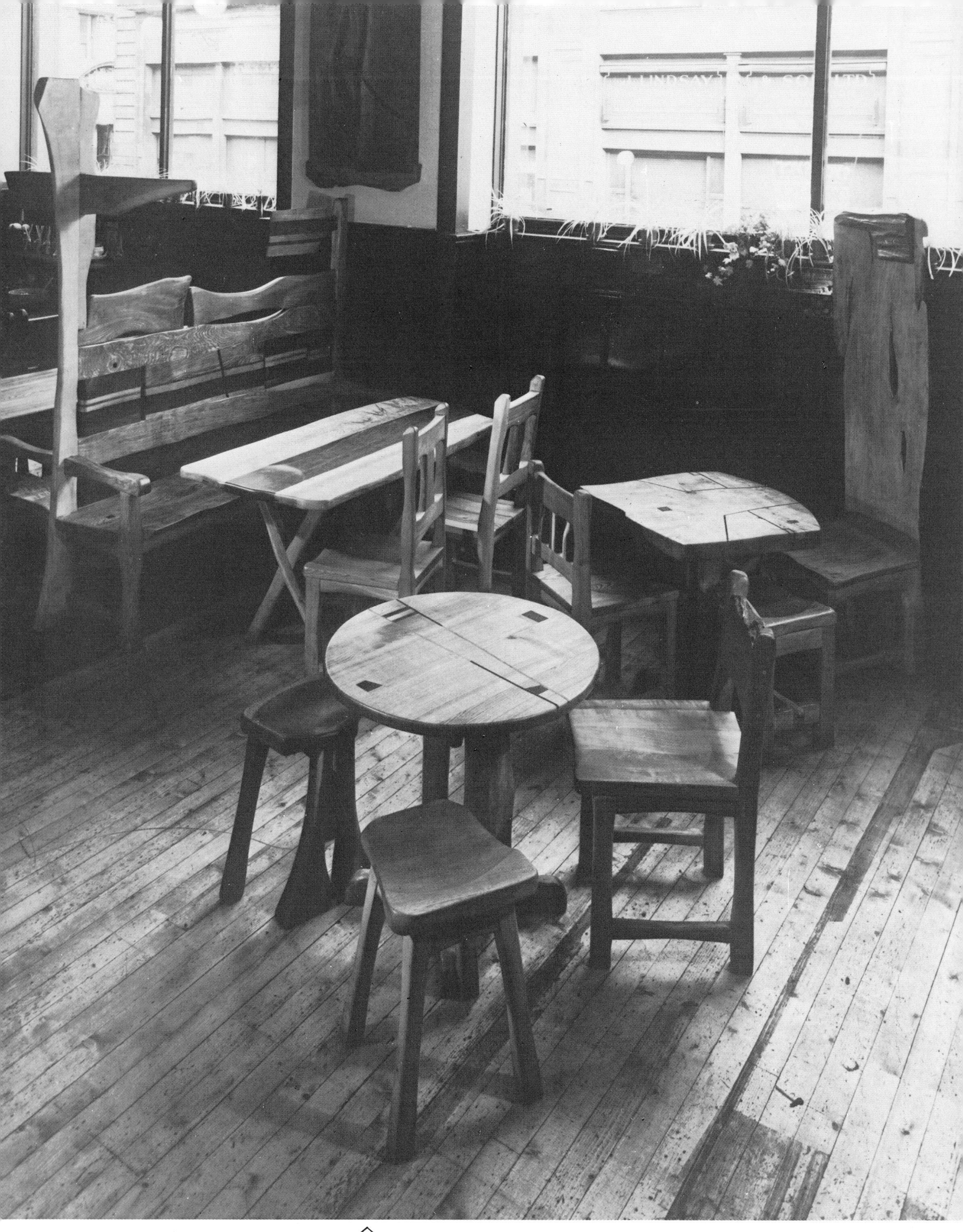

△
Tim Stead
Interior of the Cafe Gandolfo, Albion Street,
Glasgow, which was completely furnished by Tim
Stead

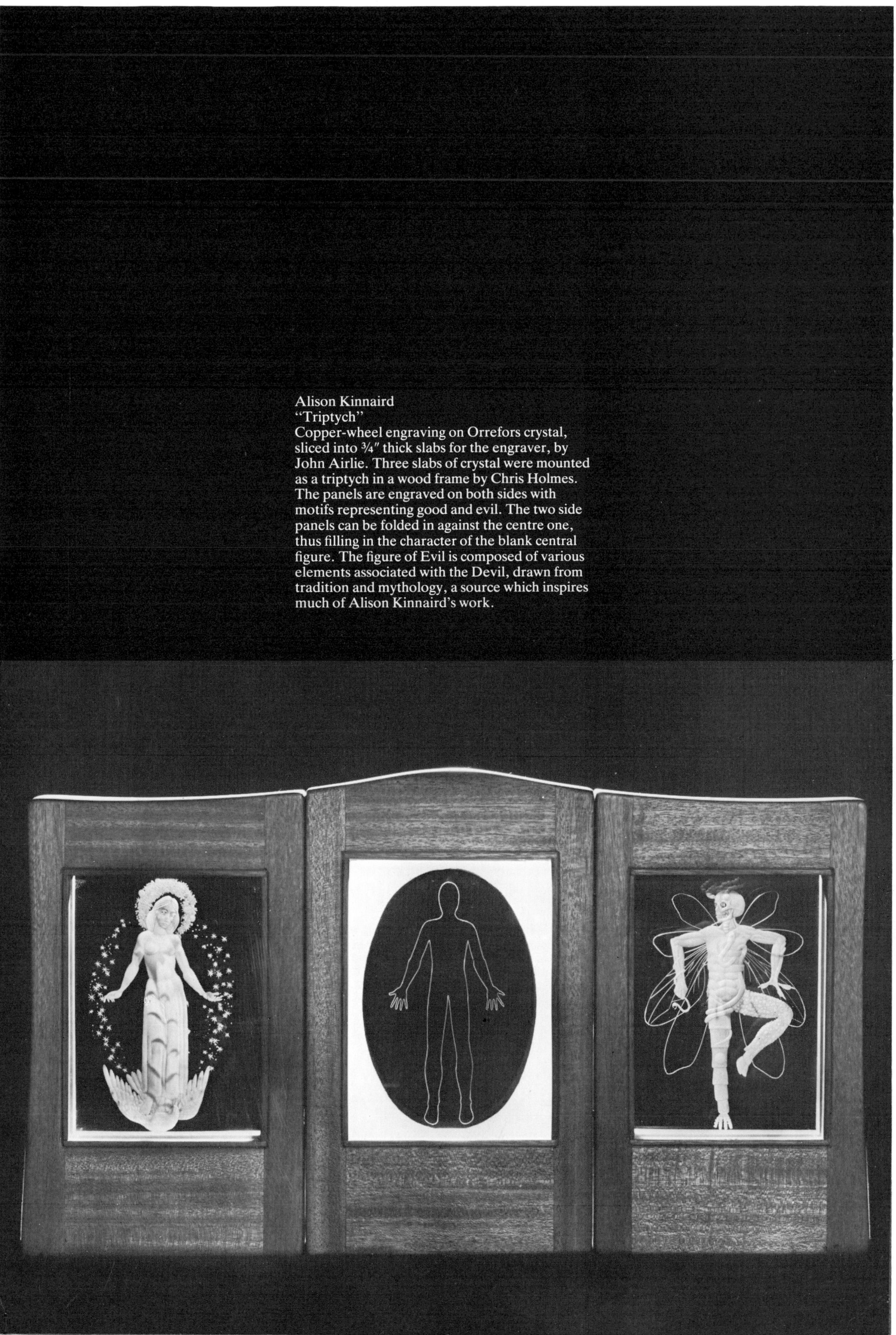

Alison Kinnaird
"Triptych"
Copper-wheel engraving on Orrefors crystal,
sliced into ¾″ thick slabs for the engraver, by
John Airlie. Three slabs of crystal were mounted
as a triptych in a wood frame by Chris Holmes.
The panels are engraved on both sides with
motifs representing good and evil. The two side
panels can be folded in against the centre one,
thus filling in the character of the blank central
figure. The figure of Evil is composed of various
elements associated with the Devil, drawn from
tradition and mythology, a source which inspires
much of Alison Kinnaird's work.

Glass has a long historical connection with Scotland, but engraving, apart from some examples of Jacobite glasses, and the influence of immigrant craftsmen from the Continent in the last century, has really only flowered in this country since the War. This striking growth is due without doubt to the establishing of a Glass Department at Edinburgh College of Art by the late Helen Monro Turner, and to her personal inspiration and example. All the engravers illustrated have been connected, directly or indirectly, with her work.

There are several techniques which may be used to engrave glass, including diamond or steel point, copper-wheel, sand-blast and acid etching. While some engravers use a combination of these methods the great proportion of Scottish engravers employ the ancient and highly-developed technique of copper-wheel engraving, using a small lathe on which can be mounted a variety of copper wheels. To these are applied grinding or polishing powders and the glass is moved against the wheel from beneath to produce the cut.

In all cases, the engraver is dependant on glass makers as the source of his material. The tradition for British crystal is that it should be cut, and the glass factories have, on the whole, been reluctant to supply engravers with the blank crystal required. Most of the glass engravers, apart from those actually working within a glass company, have thus been forced to go to the continental glass makers for supply — notably to those in Sweden. It is, therefore, very satisfactory to see in the last couple of years, a move towards closer liaison between engravers and glass makers in Scotland, not only from the larger well-established firms, but also from the small independant glass blowers, some of whom have indicated that they are willing and able to produce crystal glass of a quality suitable for engraving, and in some cases to blow special pieces to the engraver's own design. This co-operation must lead to the opening up of many new possibilities for the engraver, and an exciting future for glass engraving in Scotland in the next few years.

8 *Engraved Glass*

It is a difficult and demanding discipline, but the results have a sculptured depth and yet a delicacy which cannot be produced in any other way. Scottish engravers have gained an international reputation for the quality of their work in this field.

The engraver has the necessary limitation of the nature of the glass on which he works. The surface to be decorated is often curved, and always the transparency of the material must be taken into account. A design cannot be simply applied to any piece of glass — the object must be thought of as a whole, so that the engraving enhances the shape of the glass which carries it, and vice versa. On the other hand, the engraver may find that the shape of a particular goblet or the texture of a rough chunk of crystal, or the reflections suddenly apparent when a block of glass is moved, acts as inspiration for the subject of an engraving. Glass has its own mystical, magical character — it is illusory, it is visible yet invisible. It thus lends itself to subjects of fantasy or illusion, and many of the Scottish engravers have found this quality ideal for conjuring up the images from their own traditions of myth and legend.

Jean Murray
Set of copper-wheel engraved goblets,
Dartington Glass.
23×9 cm

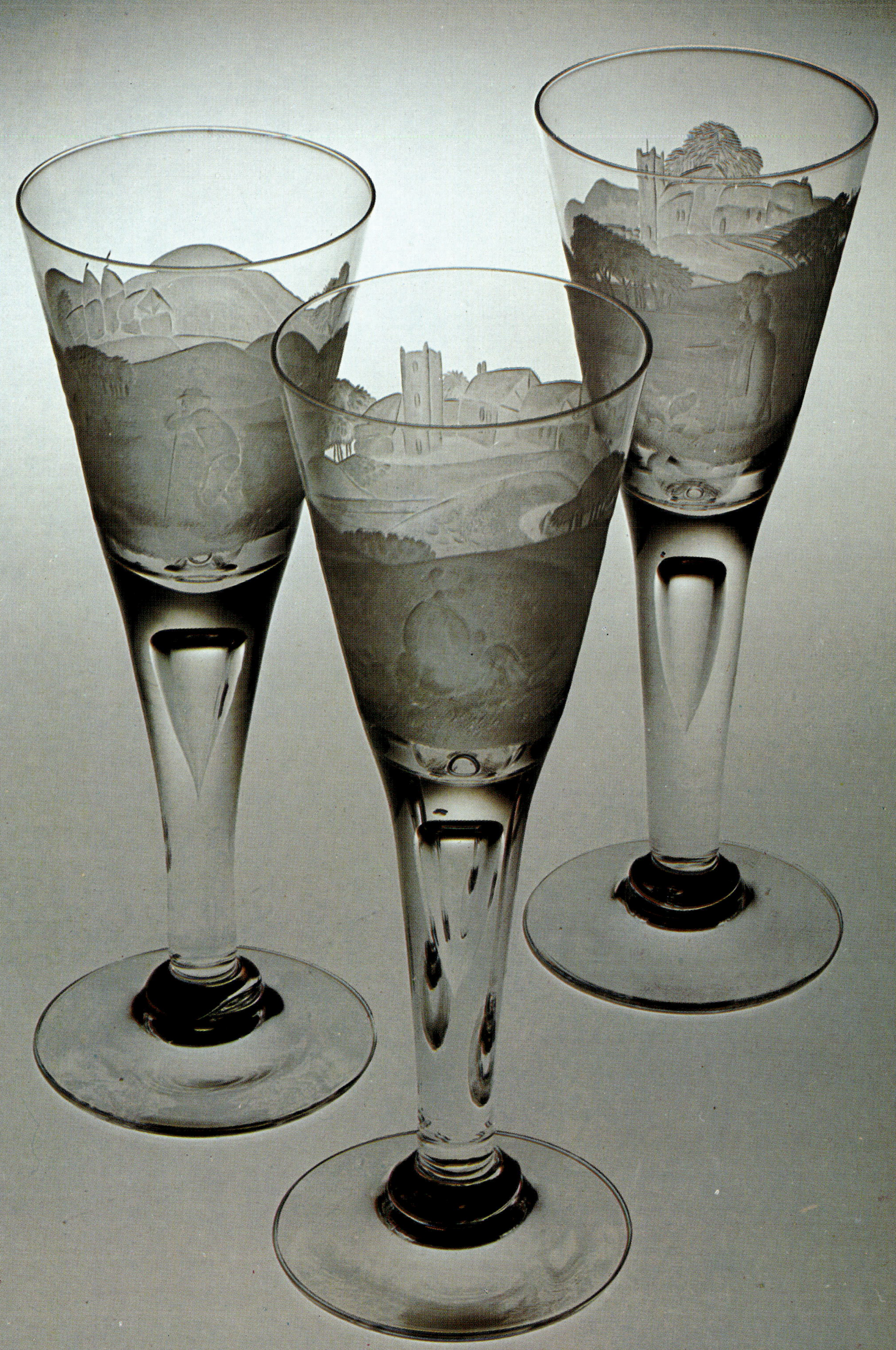

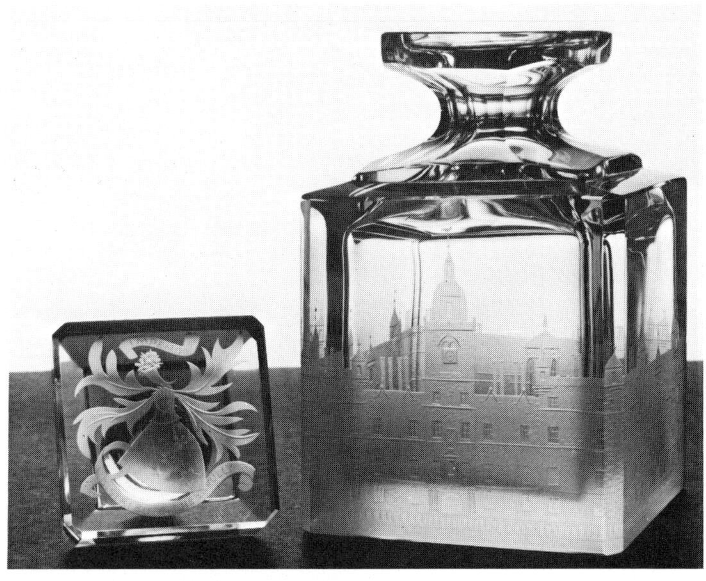

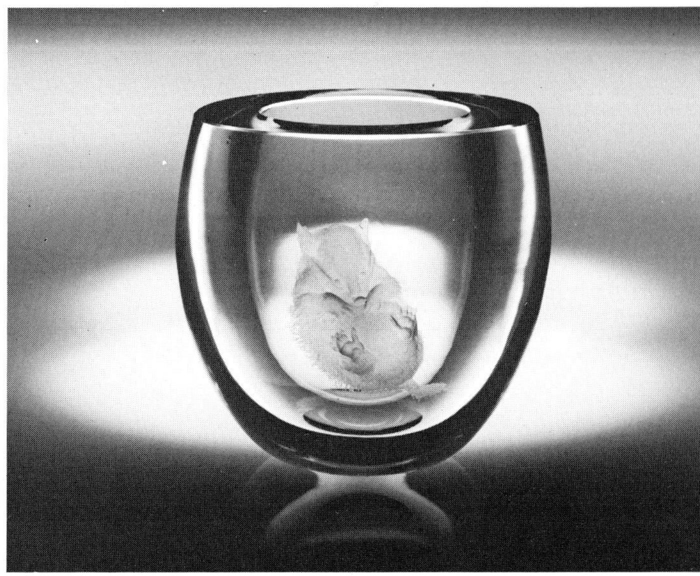

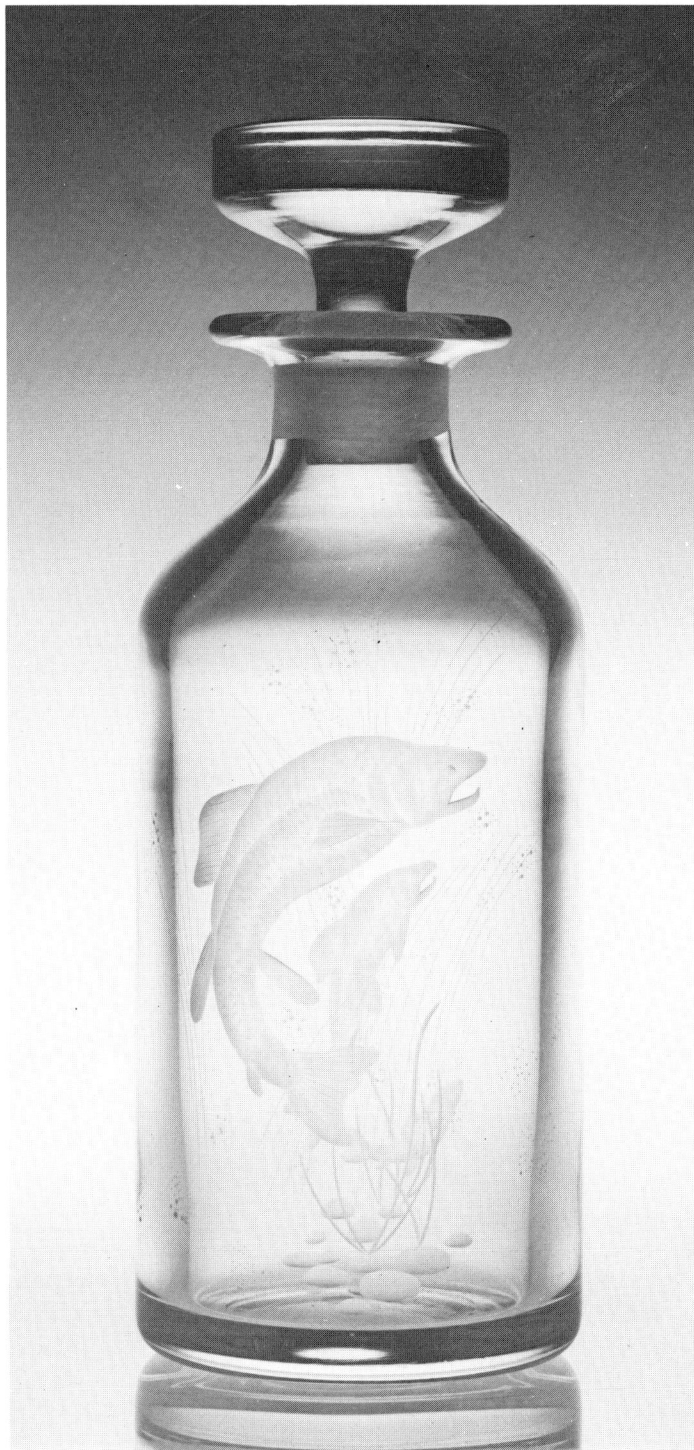

Norman Orr
"Sleeping Badger"
Copper wheel engraving on bowl
9·6 cm high×9·5 cm diameter

David Gulland
Decanter "Salmon Leap" Copper wheel
engraved design on full lead crystal decanter.
27×14 cm
Decanter—George Heriot's School, Edinburgh.
A commissioned piece employing sand blast and
copper wheel engraving techniques exploiting
the three-dimensional form of the cube.
12×12×12 cm

Denis Mann
Copper wheel engraved cubes.
"I find a fascination that's hard to explain in
playing around with these cubes. I don't want to
decorate the surface so much as encase it, or cut
into the cube so that the cube remains a piece on
it's own but with a new character."
8×8×8 cm
1. Starbright
2. Milky way

Harold Gordon
"Bison"
Copper wheel engraving on glass block

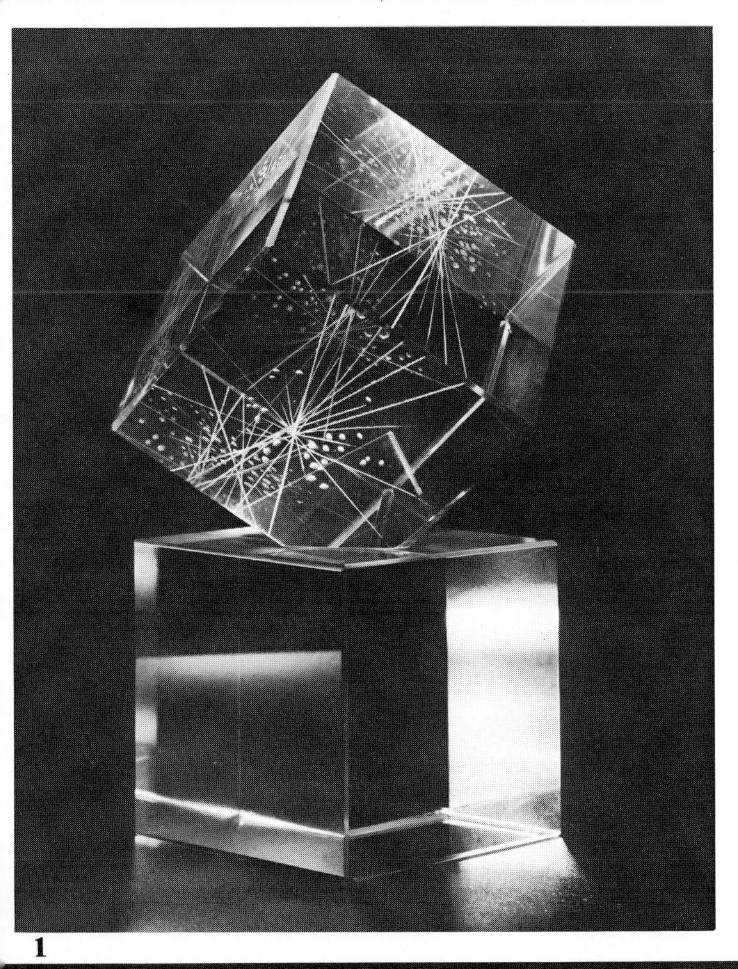

1

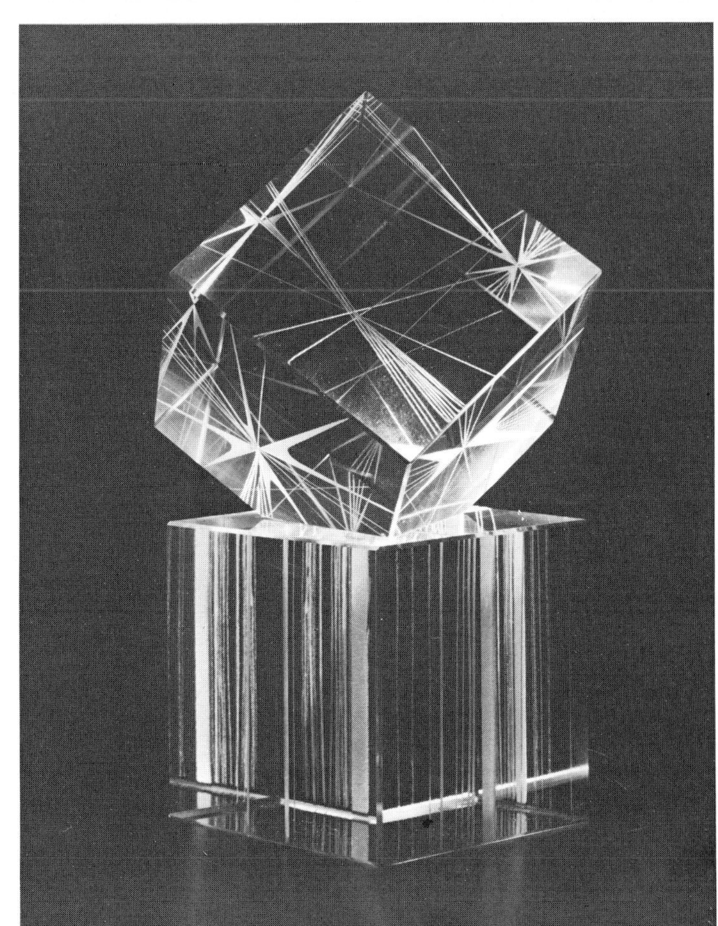

2

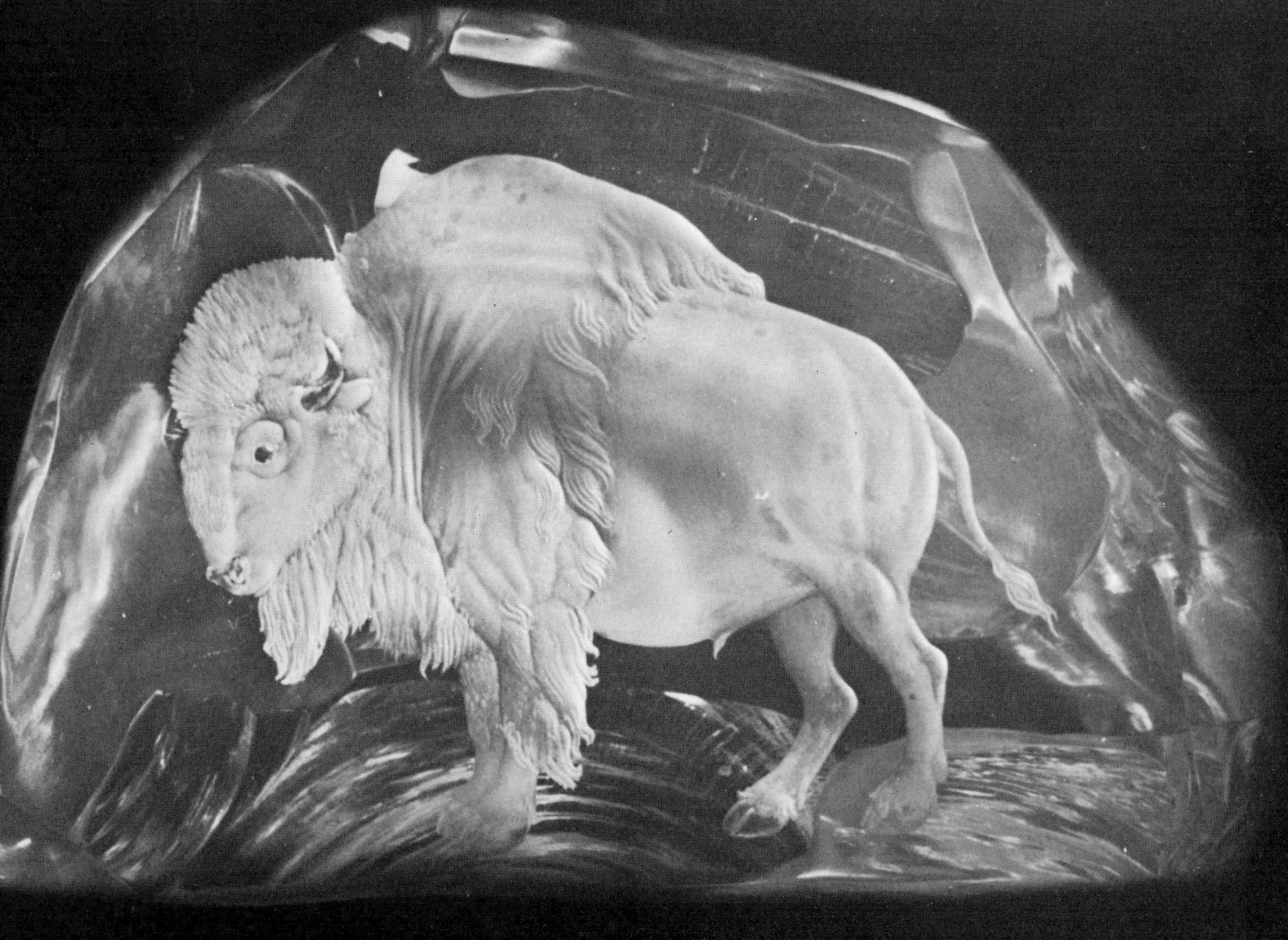

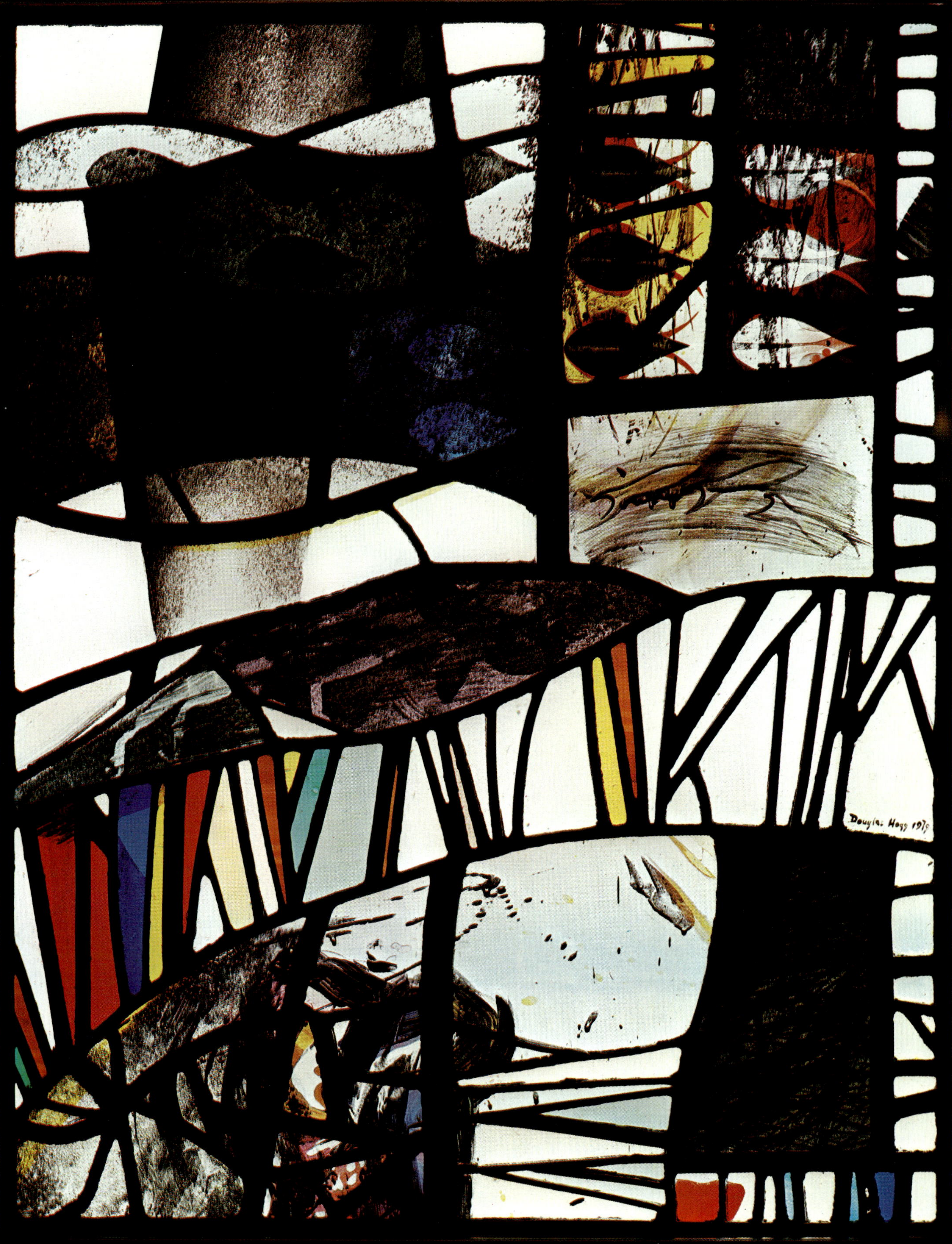

Douglas Hogg
Panel 74·0×60 cm
"My current work in stained glass is concerned
with working both 'for myself' ie drawings,
panels etc for exhibition purposes—and also
fulfilling commissions when the opportunity

9

Stained Glass

Stained glass is a medium which at its best uses glass, light, lead and architecture to convey emotion and aesthetic ideas. Sucessful design can only be based on a complete mastery of and sympathy with the processes of cutting and leading. Only if all components, glass, lead and light play their part together in comfort does the window succeed.

Over the past three centuries, and indeed in Europe still today, painters were employed to paint on glass designs originally conceived for canvas. The resulting brown and yellow, almost opaque screen owes little to the light, glass sparkle and colour to which glass is so suited. Throughout the present century in Scotland at least, the training of glass artists has been founded on an understanding of the materials of the craft; it has not attempted to impose ideas from a different medium on glass and lead.

The craft at present is in a vigorous and healthy state. Great interest is being taken in domestic and secular panels and in conservation of old glass. A course in conservation was recently introduced at Edinburgh College of Art which has given students insight into different periods of painting and glazing and different approaches to the care in the making of windows. So far the work has been restricted to glass of about 100 to 150 years old, however the course may eventually expand into the restoration of twelfth-century work.

The stained glass artists who work in Scotland fall into three groups: those aged 60-75 who have spent their entire life in this craft with great success; the younger school, aged 30 to 40 and the coming students aged 25 to 30 who are just beginning to find occasional work. Obviously the quality of glass and originality of conception comes from all groups and age matters little. One fortunate thing about working with this medium is that each window is a new idea and a fine contemporary window can and often does spring from active, lively minds.

10

Hot Glass

At present there are more than twenty glassmaking locations scattered throughout Scotland, from Wick to Castle Douglas, from Selkirk to Morar. They range in size from the one person studio to the large industrial undertakings of Edinburgh Crystal at Penicuik, to Caithness Glass at Wick, Oban and Perth. The geographical and size range is matched by the variety of products which, if not all of the highest quality, gives Scotland in the latter part of the twentieth century as lively a glass industry as at any time since the establishment of the Wemyss glasshouse in the early years of the seventeenth century.

It is a constantly changing pattern illustrating many of the traditional features of the history of glassmaking throughout Europe. Craftsmen move frequently, from industrial undertakings to small studios and vice versa; ideas and techniques spread almost as fast. Particularly in the smaller studios there is a constant search for new techniques and the rediscovery and reapplication of old. Against a general background of a revival in all forms of craft and handwork and many are especially inspired, directly or indirectly by Labino's statement in 1967 that 'research into glass compositions which will produce new, unusual, and exciting colours, techniques in the blowing of glass objects, all this is but a part of the fascinating material which can be used as a medium for art.'

A significant part in this development has been played by the Glass Department of the Edinburgh College of Art, which, in addition to reviving and developing glass engraving has encouraged experimentation in the blowing of glass forms and constructions, under John Lawrie so that the sculptural qualities of the material are exploited as in the work of Ann Fleming and Alison McConachie.

Work with hot glass ranges from the reworking of borosilicate glass, clear in the case of Sue Murray's vegetable and fungoid forms, or coloured in the case

of Frits Akerboom. In this field the most significant contribution has come from Ed Iglehart, a chemist by training, who constantly adapts or combines old and new techniques, 'heating, stretching, building, and blowing, using oxides and natural glazes for colours and decoration.'

On a slightly larger scale an older generation of experimental blowers included Ken Wainwright and John Airlie, while a newer generation includes Charles Ramsay, David Kaplan, Darryl Hinz (now working in Denmark) and Peter Layton. Their work involves the re-appraisal of the possibilities of glass either in coloured or clear, with or without applied or surface decoration.

A major development in recent years has been the establishment of

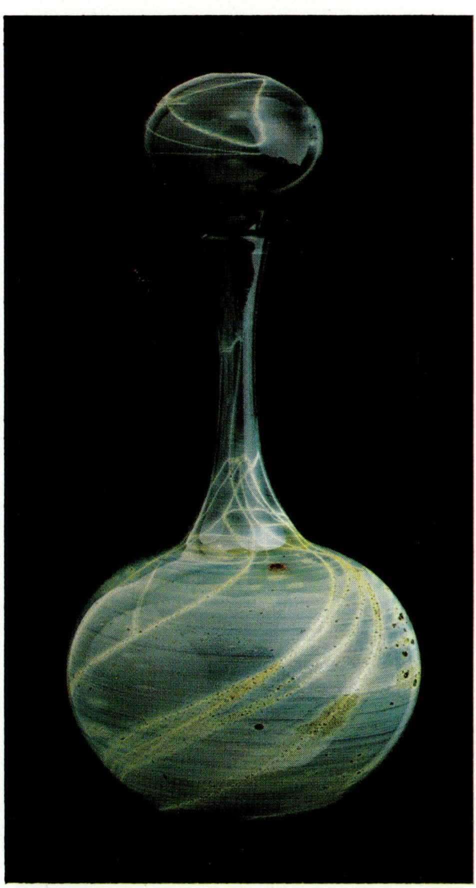

Ed Iglehart
Tall neck vase with cobalt interior and silver exterior both lamp-blown glass.
14×9 cm

paperweight making. Apart from Paul Ysart, whose family developed both Monart and Vasart glass before and after the Second World War, paperweights have never been a significant feature of the Scottish glass industry. They are now the sole product of Perthshire Paperweights and Selkirk Glass as well as forming a major part of the production of Caithness Glass and until recently Strathearn Glass. While the traditional styles are still produced with skill and originality, it is with the development of abstract designs and the exploitation of the glass itself with various inclusions whether of colour or air bubbles that Scottish makers have made a significant step forward. Colin Terris (Caithness Glass), Peter Holmes (Selkirk Glass), John Airlie, Peter Layton, Herbert Dreir, William Manson, Alistair Ross and D. MacDonald, have all contributed significantly to this field.

As with all crafts, and glassmaking at all levels is a handcraft, the problem of scale is significant. The studio glassmaker particularly is confronted with the problem of time and market — how to produce sufficient saleable material to allow time for the development of individual perhaps less marketable items. The glassmaker has yet to be accepted as fully as the potter as part of the craft or art scene but the variety of work being carried out in Scotland at present gives hope for the future.

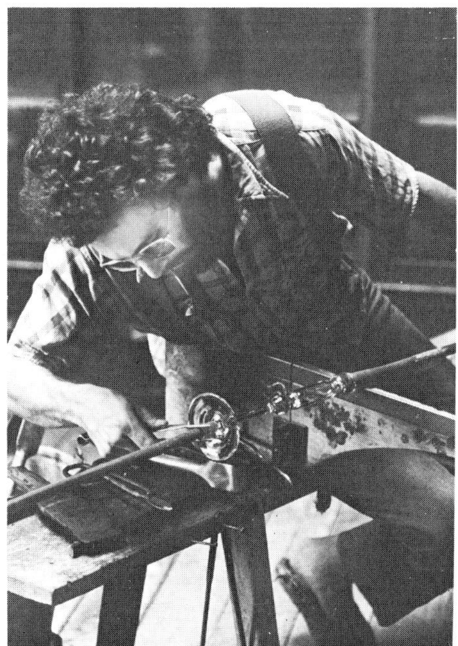

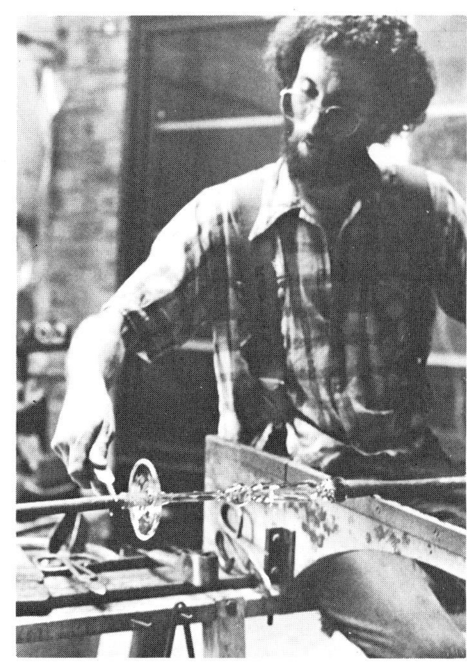

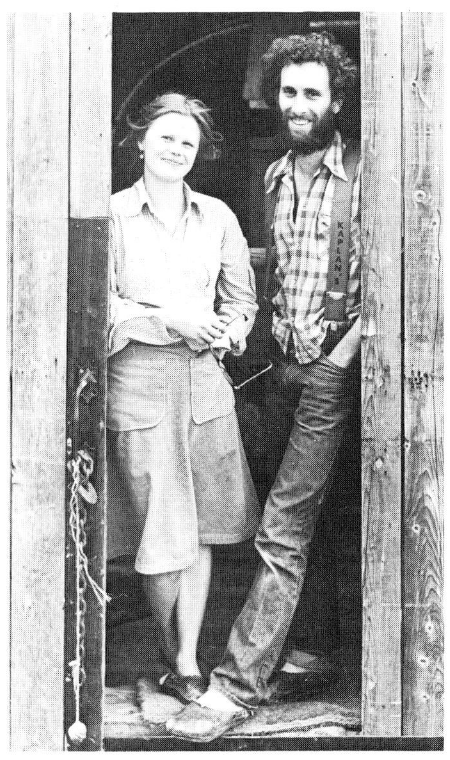

Lindean Mill Glass is made by Annica Sandstrom and David Kaplan, and the workshop has been in existence since June 1978.
Annica and David are making glass to their own designs, using traditional Scandinavian glassmaking techniques. The glasses are completely handmade and hand finished.
After having made a goblet by attaching a stem and foot to the blown "bowl" of the goblet, the piece is separated from the blowing iron. This is done by connecting a steel rod (pontil rod) to the foot of the goblet. The rim of the glass can then be tooled to the desired shape.
This process produces a strong, rounded rim and also a "pontil mark" showing where the pontil rod has been attached to the foot. This mark is not polished but is left to show that the glass is a genuine handmade article.

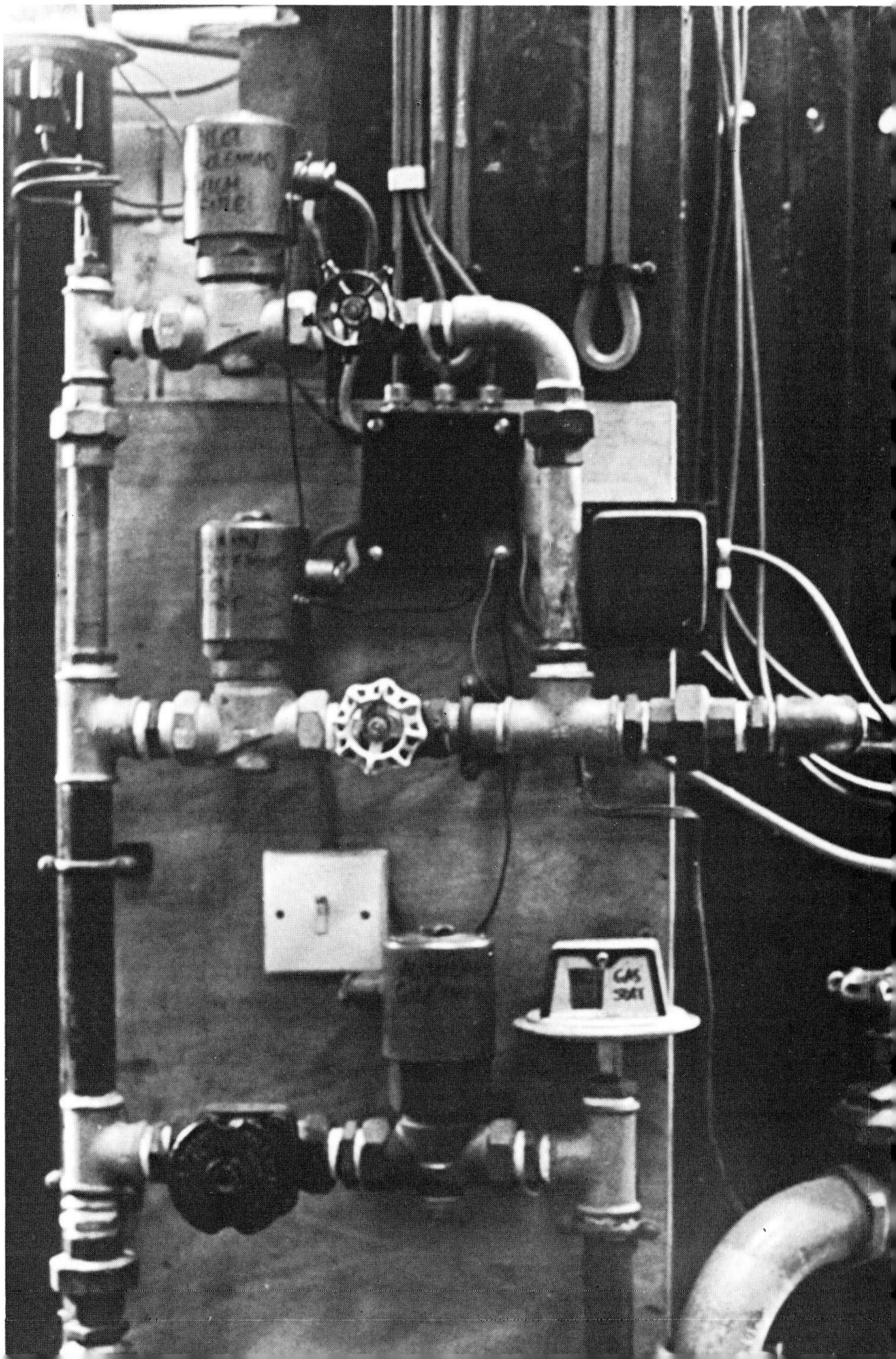

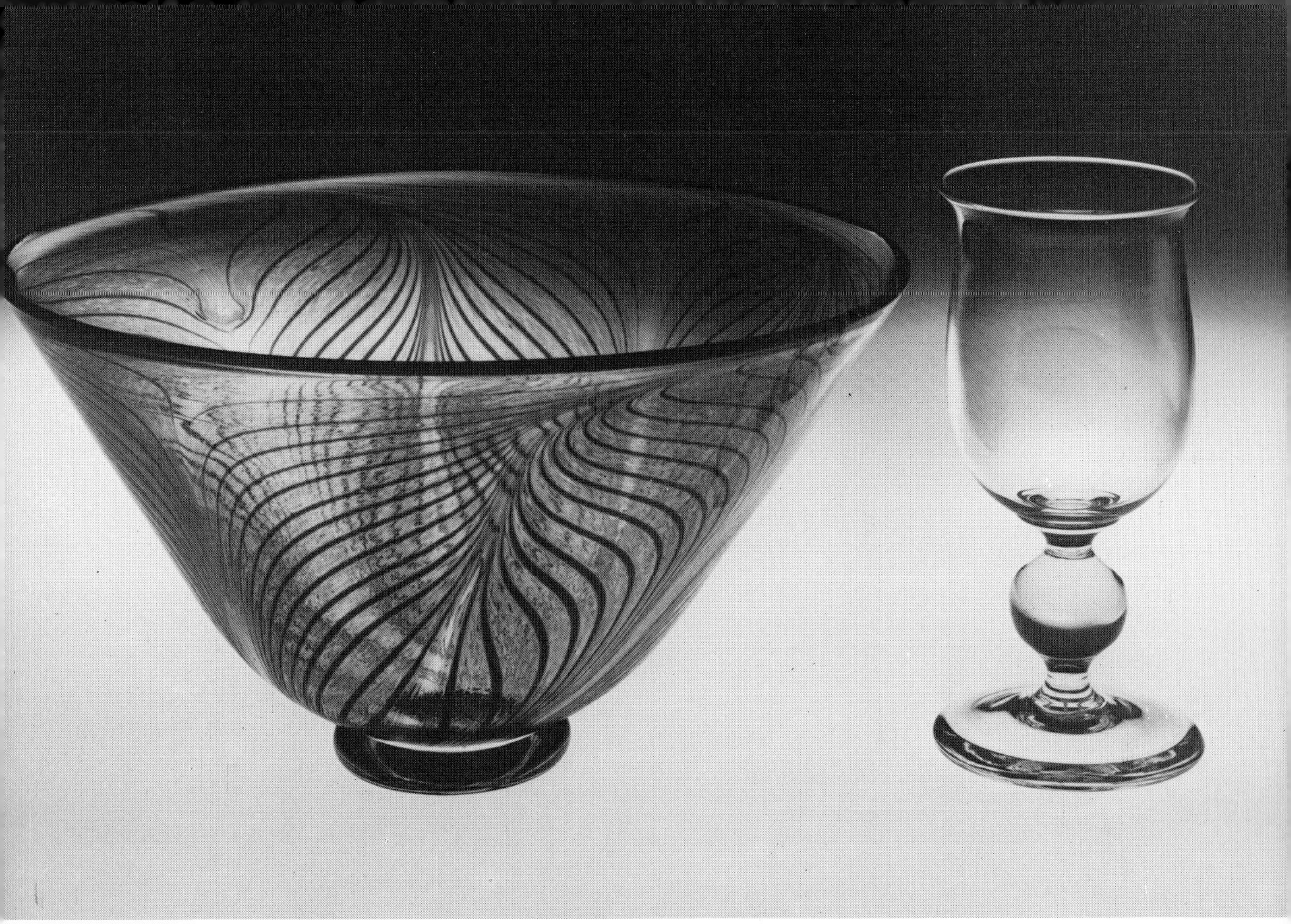

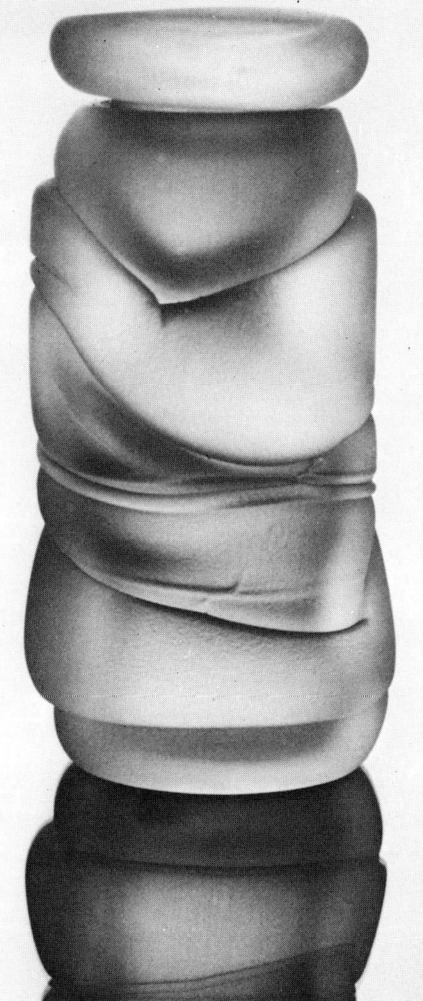

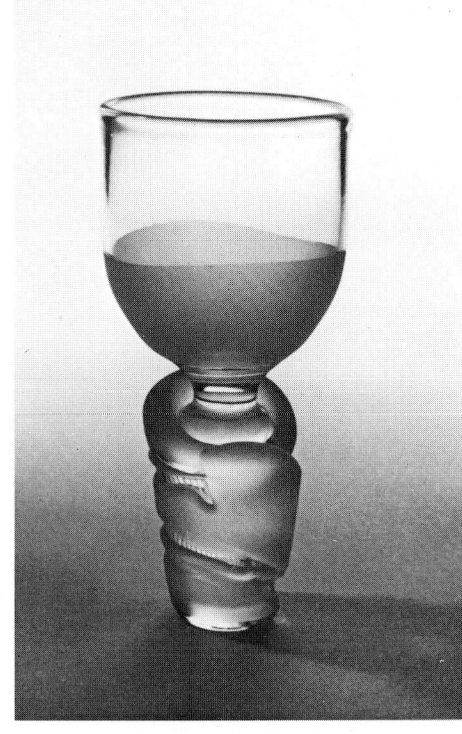

△
Lindean Mill Glass
Bowl and Goblet
25 cm diameter×9 cm

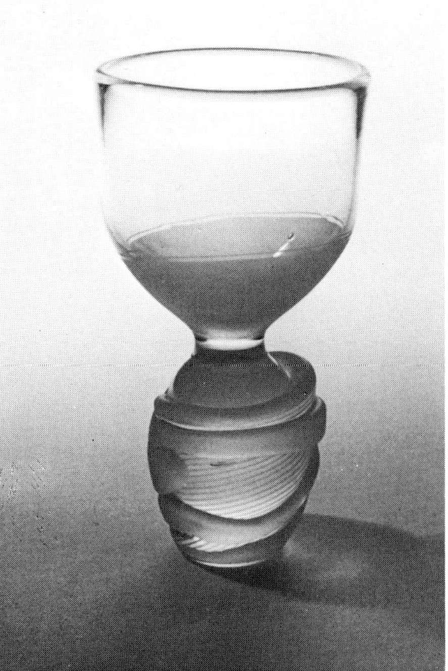

▽
Alison Maconachie
wrapped stem goblets, with sand-blasted detail c.
12 cm high
cut and sand blasted bottle 14 cm high

The last decade has seen a steadily increasing interest in the crafts of gold and silversmithing and of jewellery-making, as can be seen by the numbers of young people wishing to enter instruction and by the demand from the general public for jewellery and silver other than that traditionally made available by the High Street retail jeweller. There has developed an increasing awareness of changing design and of the steadily widening repertoire of materials and processes, and a gradual elimination of the mysteries surrounding the jewellers' and silversmiths' craft.

The absence in Scotland of a strong centralised jewellery manufacturing base such as exists in London or Birmingham has meant that for some time the training of the majority of our jewellers and silversmiths has been the responsibility of the art colleges. While having obvious shortcomings technically, such as the lack of access to the wide variety of highly skilled and traditionally trained expert personnel available in the south, this form of education does have the advantage of offering students the chance to develop their skills and design abilities in a creative environment free from the constraints of 'trade' practice. Courses, however, are in no way insular in their

metals and other materials used in various technical applications has encouraged craftsmen to experiment more and as a result, adapt his or her approach to design and construction techniques. Thus we see the use of refractory metals such as titanium, niobium and tantalum used to good effect in a highly decorative way, we see the use of experimental alloys, while the wide range of plastics materials available is imaginatively used and is free of the associations of 'cheapness' it had not so long ago. Photo-etching on precious metal, using techniques developed for the production of printed circuits in the electronics industry is now fairly commonplace in jewellery manufacture, allowing great freedom in the design and range of surface texture, pattern and image, permitting these images to be produced in considerable quantities while simulating techniques which would have previously required great skill to execute by hand. But while these new materials and processes are available to the craftsman, they often need expensive equipment and are therefore used more successfully not in the workshops of individuals but in manufacturing units with higher outputs.

II *Jewellery*

approach and students are constantly made aware of international developments and trends in their area of study and there would appear to be no obvious 'Scottish Style'. Work of graduates is strongly individual and contemporary Scottish jewellers and silversmiths are becoming increasingly known throughout Britain and abroad. But the most encouraging trend is that more craftsmen and designers are finding it possible to continue to work in Scotland, it being no longer necessary to move south to find opportunities to pursue their craft.

The introduction of new materials and processes, mostly the result of research and development in high technology industries have also widened the scope of possibilities for the artist-craftsman. The steady (and recently alarming) rises in the costs of precious metals combined with the increasing availability of other rarer

The simple artist-craftsman by definition exists in what must be a labour — or skill — intensive area and the hand techniques which he or she uses are usually difficult, if not impossible, to reproduce by any other method, nor is it normally the intention to produce works in large numbers. Each piece is an individual statement of their own creativity and laboriously acquired technical skill, and, ideally, one which transcends the intrinsic value of the precious or other materials with which it is made. In fact, it is becoming increasingly apparent that the buying public are beginning to purchase hand-made jewellery with less regard for its bullion value, as well as realising that privately commissioned works in gold and silver are less expensive than might be expected.

Anne Finlay
Top Armband
Acrylic, polyester resin, silk threads.
Three aluminium armbands
inset
Brooches in silver, acrylic, one with brightly coloured wrapped silk threads, others with quilted satin and threads, pierced aluminium polyester resin and acrylic.

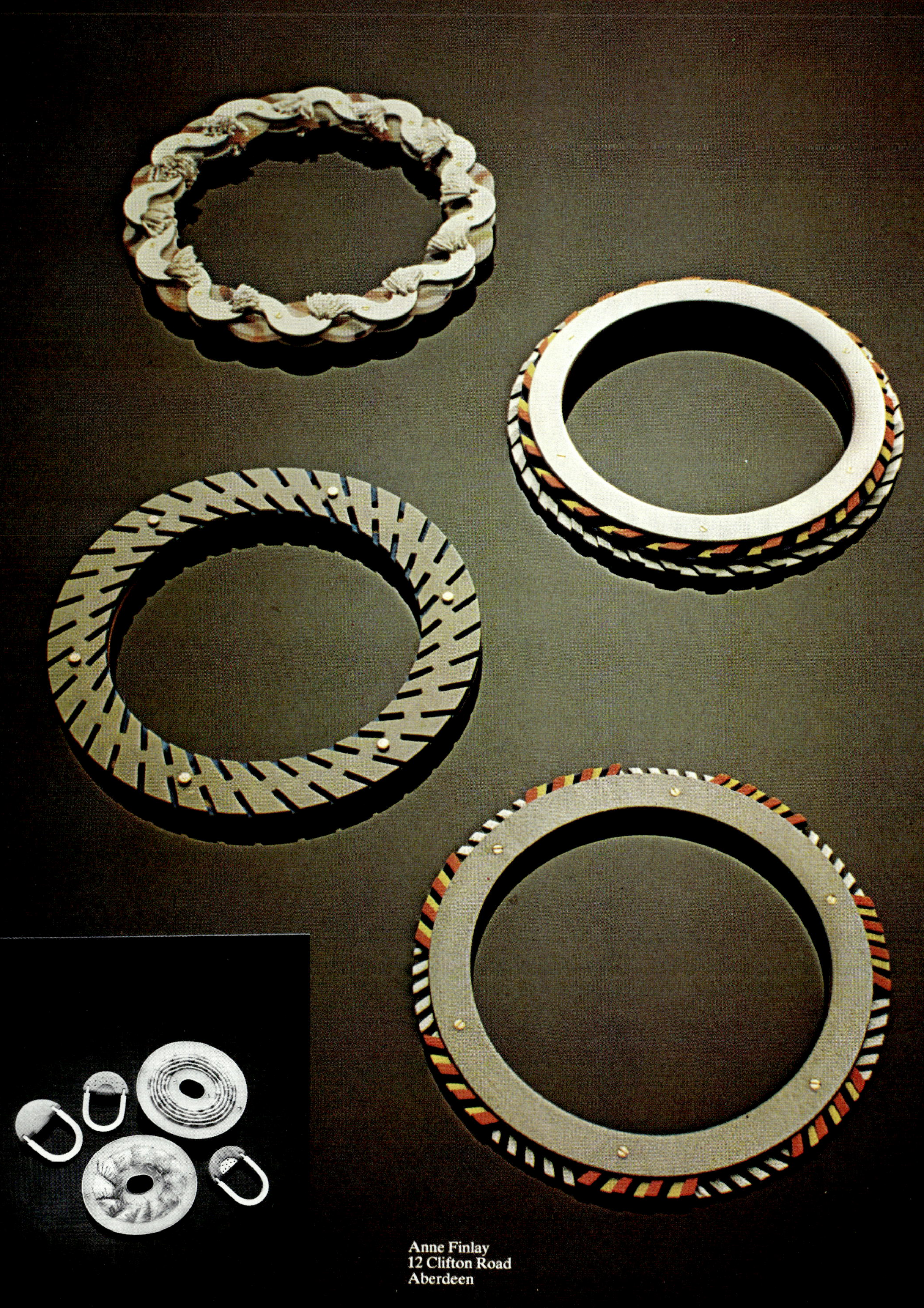

Anne Finlay
12 Clifton Road
Aberdeen

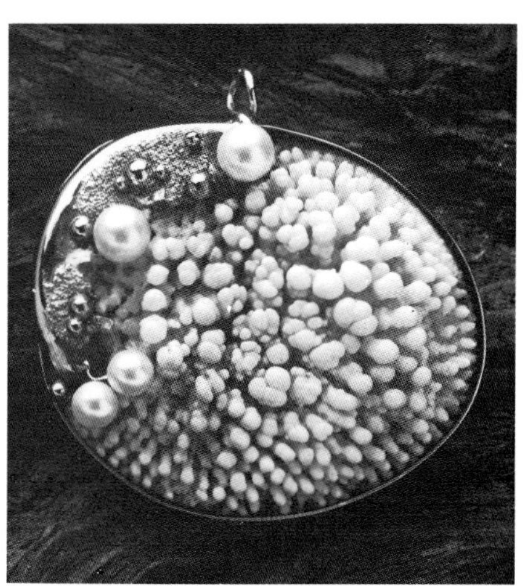

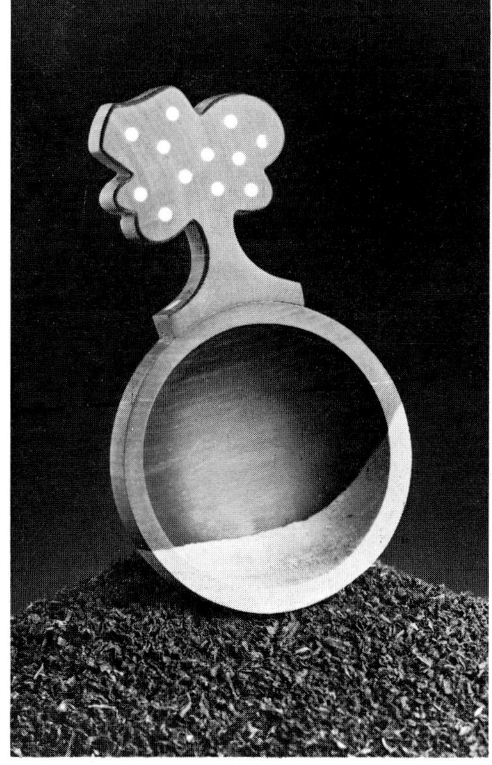

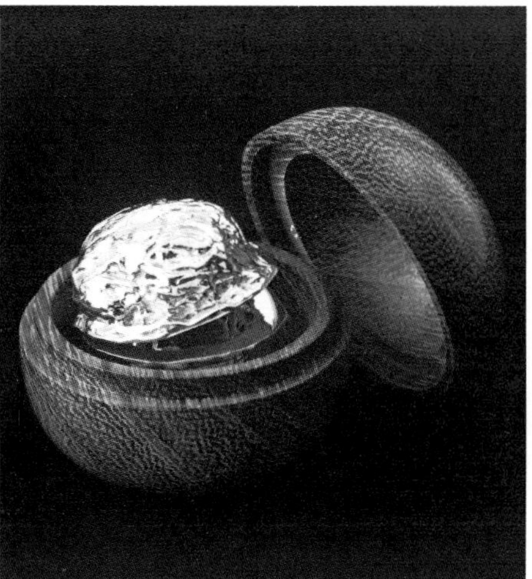

Ruby necklace in 9 ct gold
The necklace, made from 9 ct gold, and shell with a pinkish cast, is set with seven rubies. It is an articulating piece which also has areas of granulated and reticulated gold.
13 cm O.A.

Double-sided coral/shell pearl and 9 ct gold:
The pendant was designed to be viewed from either side and is constructed from 9 ct gold, coral on shell and cultured pearls. The coral-covered shell was an accidental find in an antique shop and greatly influenced the eventual shape of the piece.
4·2 cm diameter.

Francesca Porrelli
Silver walnut shell box with hinge
This silver box is a lost-wax casting. An actual walnut shell generated the master pattern through 3 stages of moulding and casting. Such techniques enable accurate copies of many natural objects.
It weighs 3 ounces and its two rims are contoured into one another as in the natural state.
5·5×5 cm

Ebony tea-caddy spoon showing both heartwood and sapwood. The tree shaped top of the spoon is decorated with silver and pinned to the bowl.
6·7 cm long

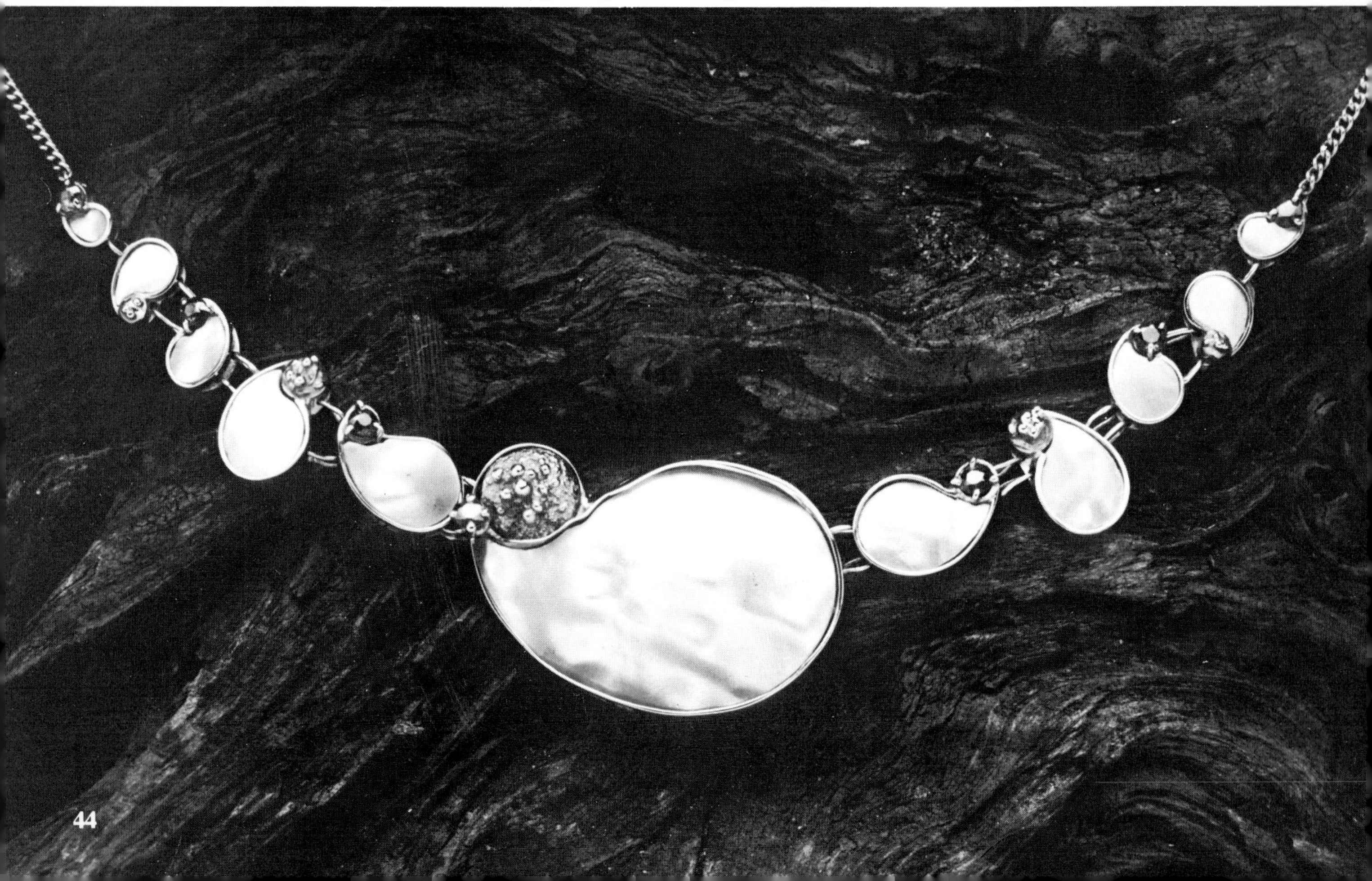

Ann Marie Shillito
Ring in silver, 9 ct gold and anodised *tantalum,*
one of a series. Manufacturing processes: 1.
Milling—three slots at angles were milled across
the top edges of a silver/tantalum/silver
sandwich. 2. Fabrication—gold bars were
soldered across the top into the slots milled in the
silver.
3. Anodising—the tantalum section was anodised
electrolytically. 4. The tantalum was finally

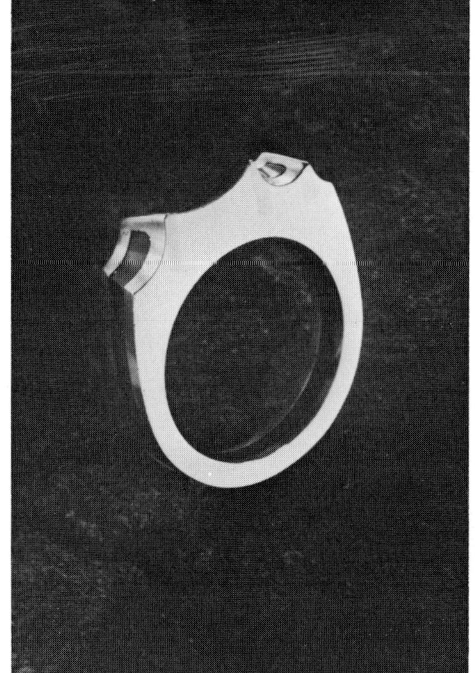

slotted up between the silver sides and onto the
gold bars. It is held in by pressure and can be
removed to be coloured differently.
2·2 cm diam.

Dorothy Hogg
Brooch in silver and gold
6×4·5 cm

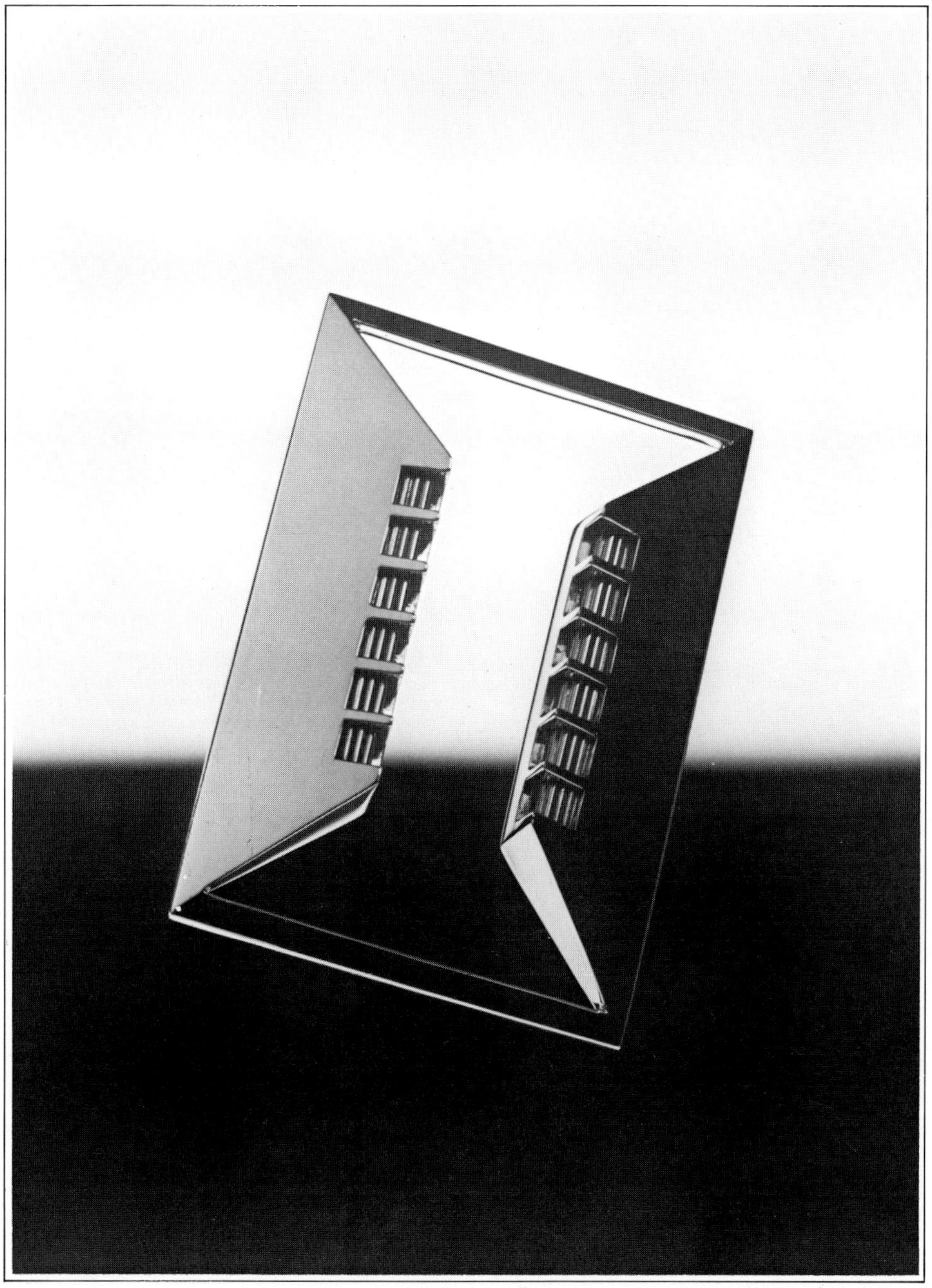

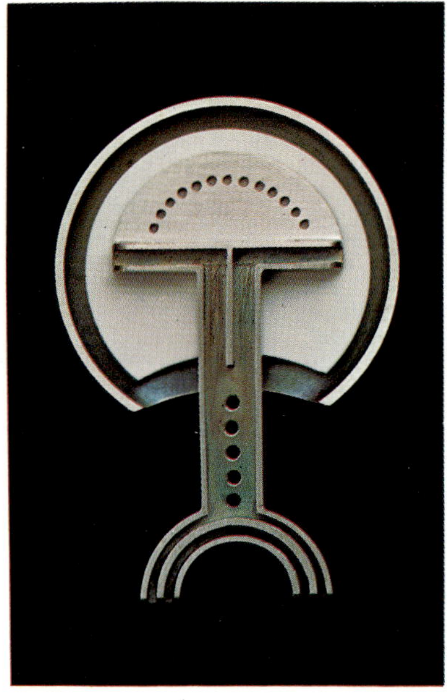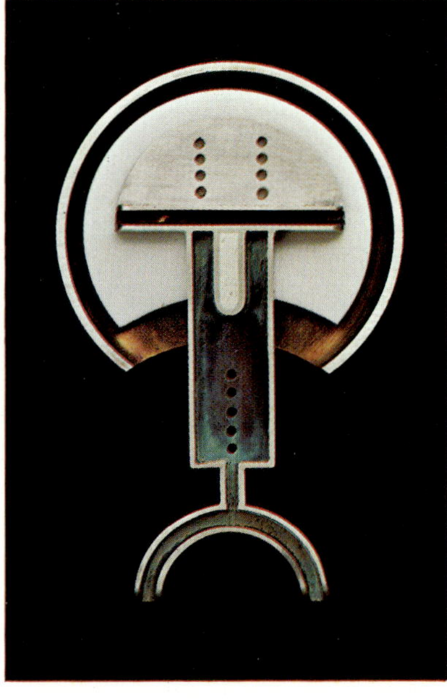

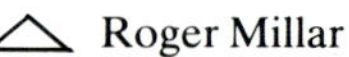 Roger Millar
Two brooches in oxidised silver and white acrylic

Eric Spiller
two brooches—aluminium, acrylic, and polyester resins
Eric Spiller's brooches come to life when they are worn. Beneath a precision constructed grid of acrylic slats, he introduces coloured resin strips and by mathematically controlling the interval and angle between each strip intriguing optical effects are produced. The result is an illusion of movement within the brooch although there are no moving parts.
All the inherent characteristics of these materials which are relatively new to jewellery making are explored to produce work of subtlety.

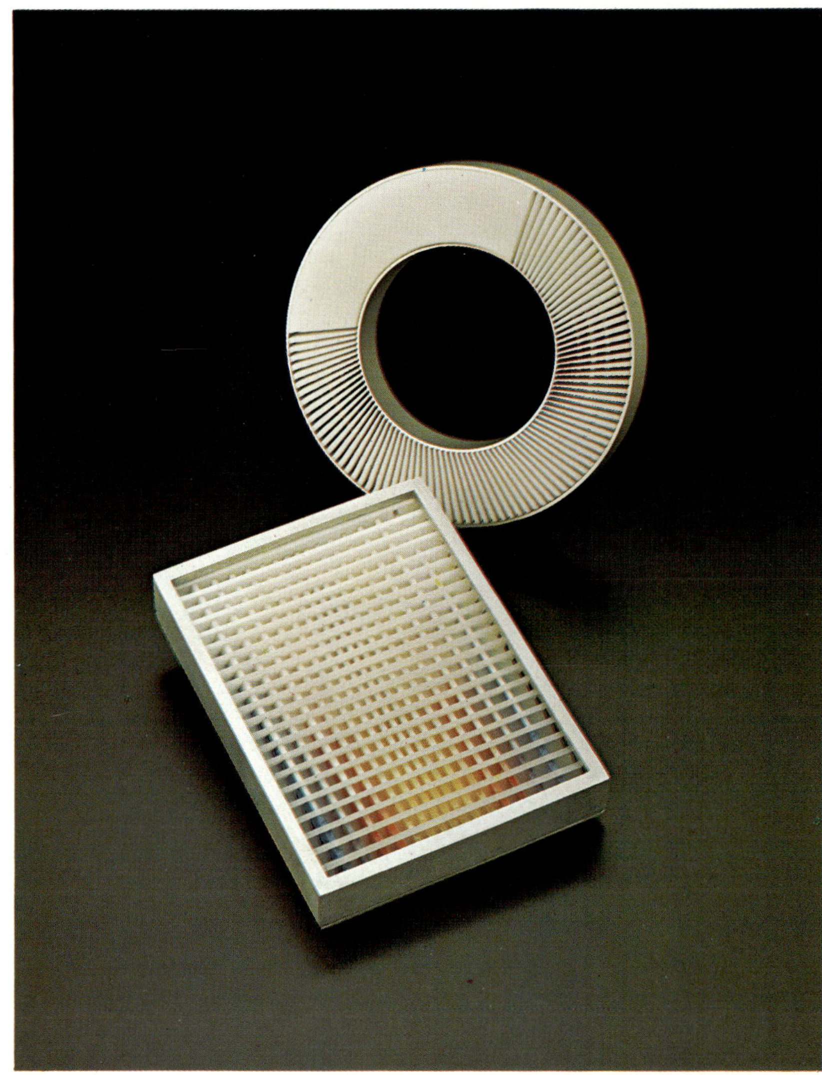

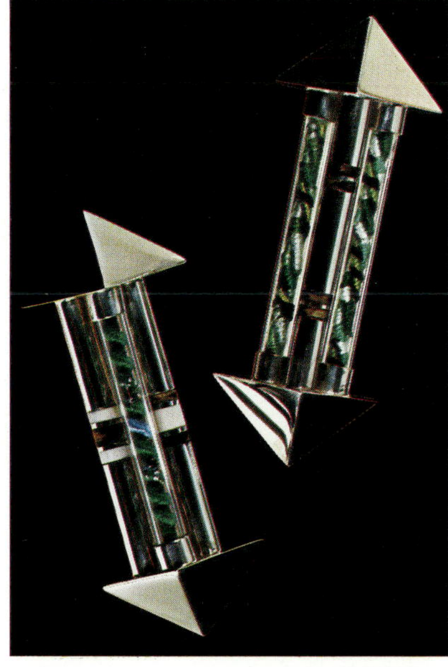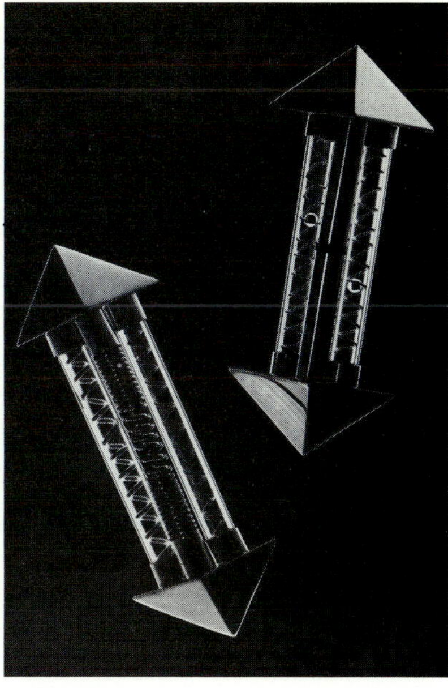

Jack Cunningham
Four brooches
Silver, acrylic, ivory, tortoishell, silks and small beads of glass or coral are combined in these brooches.
9×3·2 cm

Graham Crimmins
Pendant in silver and titanium
Graham Crimmins began to experiment with titanium while at college in Birmingham, using it as a single colour, blue, in contrast to highly polished silver. At this time titanium was already widely used in engineering and scientific fields but not much as a decorative material. He gradually realised the full potential of titanium as well as the drawbacks . . . it is barely malleable, impossible to solder and extremely difficult to form using normal silversmithing methods.
The first pieces were a series of round brooches built up of layers of different colours. The colour was achieved by using heat applied with a small gas torch directly onto the surface of the metal, the colour varying in proportion to the temperature. His latest pieces employ a technique of obtaining several colours on a single layer, still using a gas torch to colour the titanium.
5×5 cm

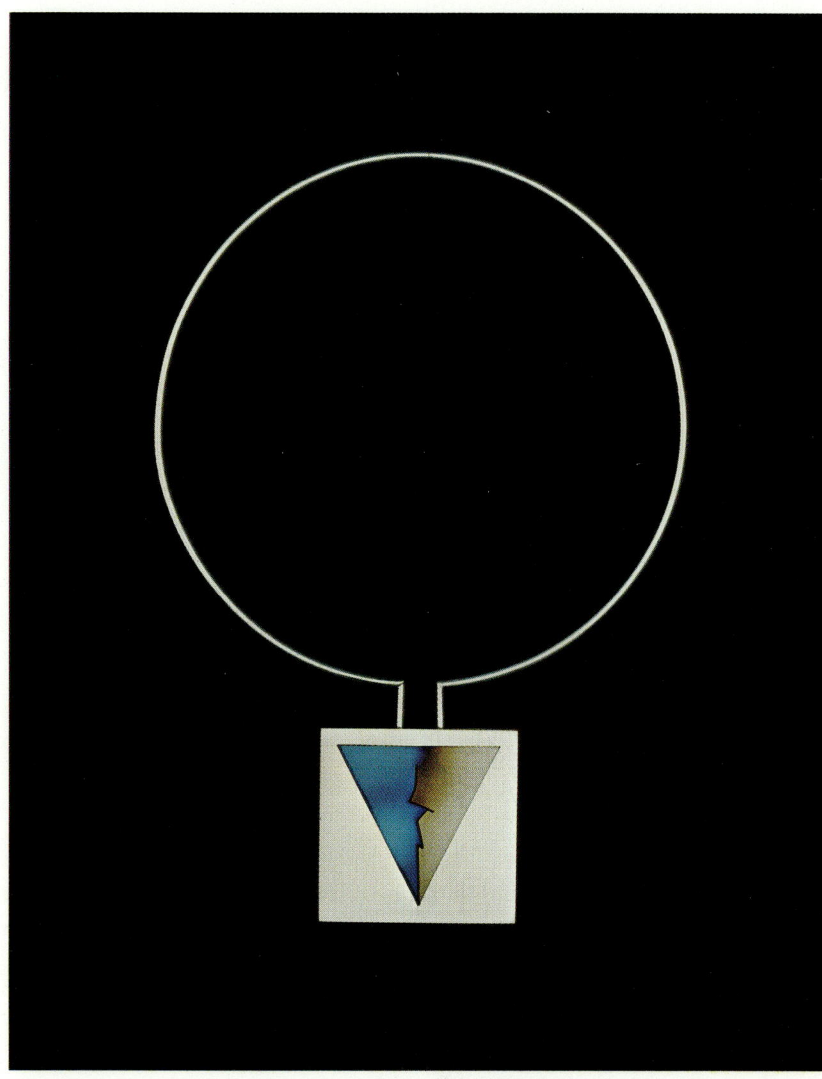

12

Silversmithing

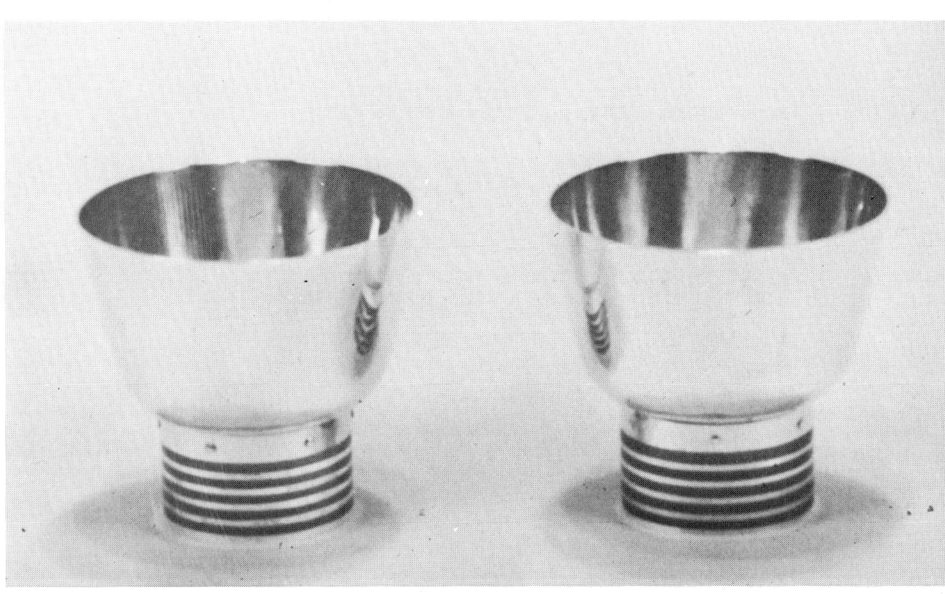

Scotland's tradition of fine silverware is a long one, and by the end of the eighteenth century, many small businesses flourished from the Borders north to Inverness. However, with the end of the 1700's appeared the first evidence of mass production. In Scotland as in England, trade came to be centralised, until finally with one or two exceptions, the majority of work in Scottish retail outlets was manufactured south of the Border. This pattern continued until the end of the nineteenth century, when a revolt against the apparent sterility of the machine-made article induced a revival of the designer craftsman.

Thus by the beginning of the last War, alongside the Trade, turning out quantities of relatively cheap, mass produced silverware, were a few highly trained specialists working principally on commissioned civic and ecclesiastical plate, though making a living in most cases by teaching in the colleges of Art.

The initial impetus came from the jeweller, but the silversmith was coming into the picture. The problem, as always was the high costs involved in setting up a workshop capable of turning out the range of work a silversmith may be called upon to make. Unlike the jeweller who can, and not infrequently has, started his business on the kitchen table, the smith must face the fact that the metal stakes and formers on which he shapes his wares will run into several hundred-weights, the duplication of small work necessitates a spinning lathe, and the hearth, brazing torch, acid baths, polishing equipment, etc will all be on a bigger scale. The inevitable need is for a large workshop, and much more capital.

The fact that the latter became available must be largely due to the special financial help given to craftsmen by the Government. However, it was the proliferation of small private galleries and craft retail outlets that kept the best and most businesslike craftsmen in business.

There was a radical change in the design of silverware after the last War. Plate, probably because of its higher material cost and generally more functional nature, tended however to be less experimental. Historically, silverware has always been slow to follow fashion. Not perhaps so surprising, when it is remembered that a customer's plate was often melted down to supply the next piece: a custom we may soon have to revive.

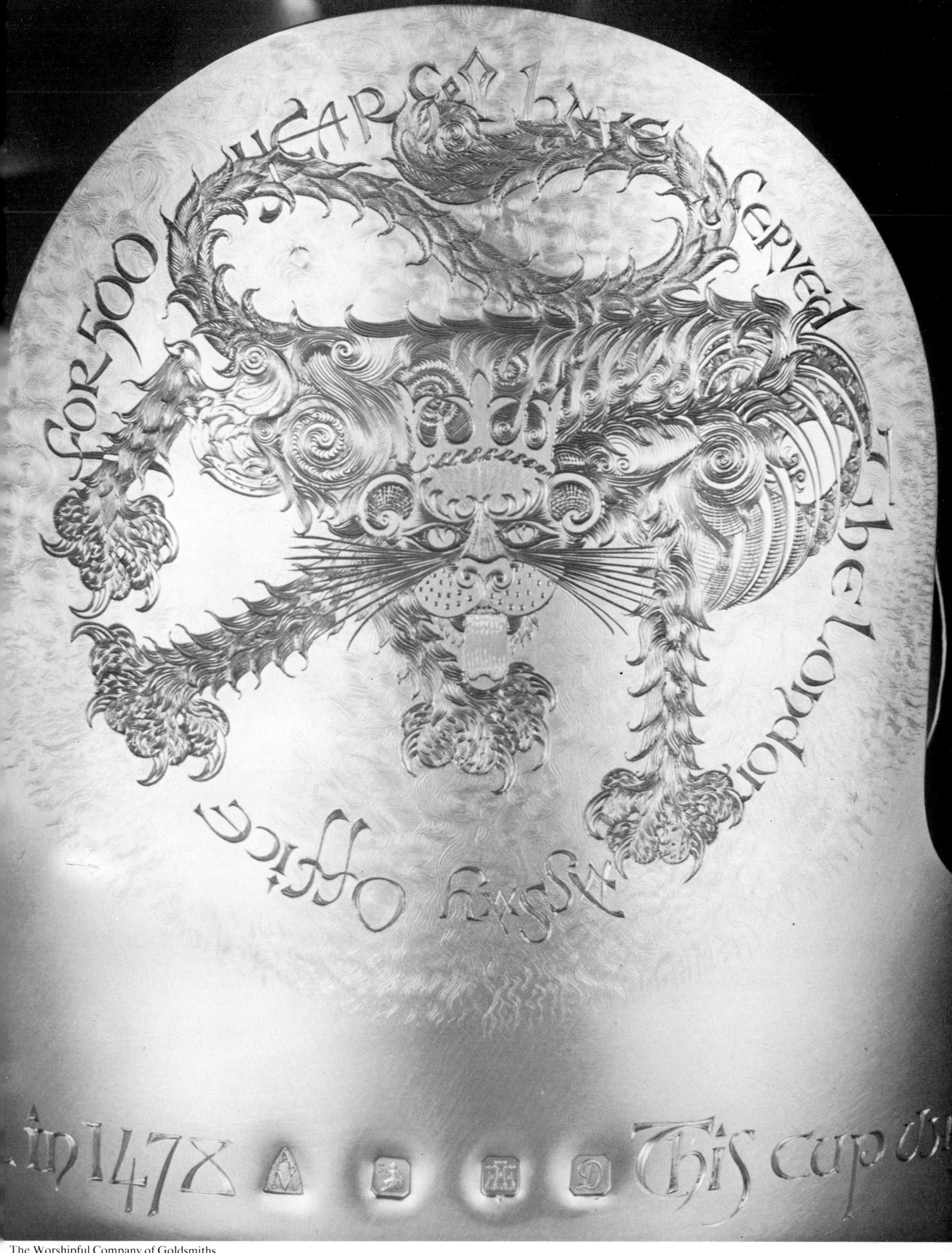

The Worshipful Company of Goldsmiths
David J F Hodge
Silver cups
The small cups are hammered from a disc, the base made from a strip of silver, soldered into a ring, turned on the lathe and enamelled. The base is attached to the cup with small handmade silver screws.
Malcolm Appelby Quincentenary Hallmarking bowl, 1978 (detail).
"I have served the London Assay Office for 500 years"
Made for the Worshipful Company of Goldsmiths, and reproduced with their permission.
Designed and engraved by Malcolm Appleby.
Made by Peter Musgrave.

The end of the 1970's saw the same verve and inventiveness that characterised the work of the jeweller being applied to the manufacture of small silverwork, coming from what might be called the middle ground craftsmen, who make their living probably from the production of jewellery, but also making a range of small work such as quaichs, tumblers and boxes.

Samuel Pepys notes in his diary that when buying a pair of candlesticks he was charged as much per ounce for fashioning them, as he was for the silver used. Excluding overheads and retail mark-up, the same has applied for the last few years. Now there is a massive increase in the cost of the material, and it is likely to affect the future.

The special one-off piece may be less in demand, but because of the prestige, money will still be found to commission it. When shortage and cost affected the use of silver in earlier centuries, a change to thinner sheet resulted. Chased and embossed decoration, fluting and hollow sections, stiffened with various filling materials, were all carefully designed to strengthen the article. Today in that area in which the craftworker operates, similar solutions will be found. Stamping and pressing in particular will take the place of much of the casting in vogue today. The precious metals will have to be looked at afresh, used sparingly, and their particular properties utilised to the full.

Inevitably prices must rise steeply. Whether or not the silversmith will be priced out of the market remains to be seen. It will be a pity if the small flame that arose from the embers at the close of the last decade prove to be just a final flare, preceeding his extinction in the next.

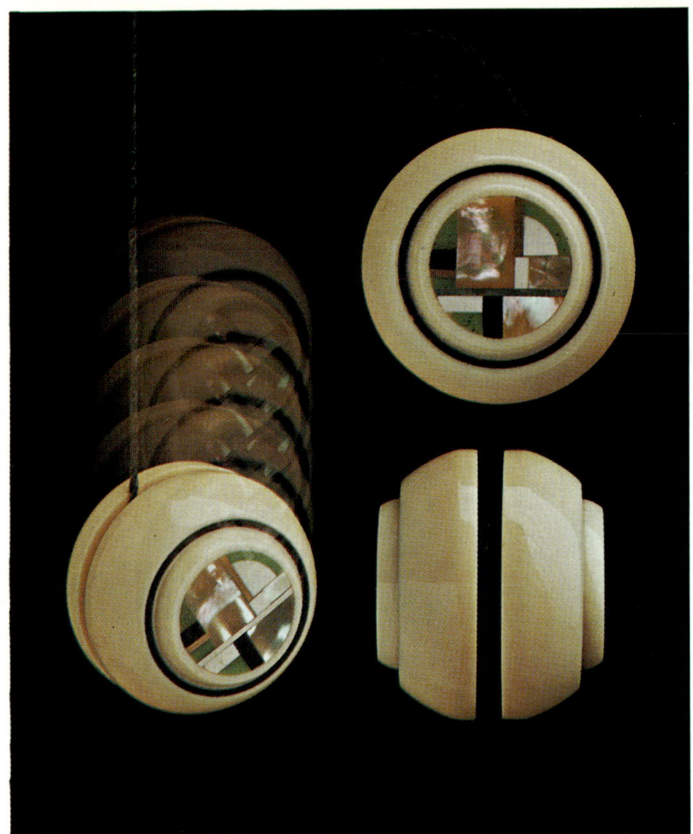

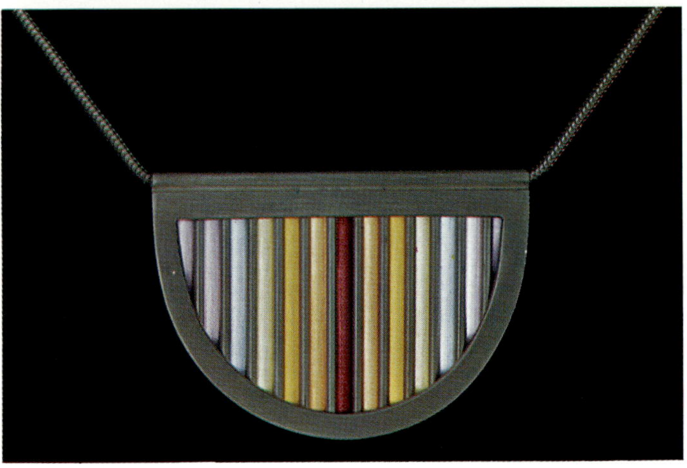

Rachel Mackie
Yo-yo
This yo-yo was lathed turned in two identical halves from a slightly damaged billiard ball. It is inlaid with resin bars, tortoishell (recycled) and mother-of-pearl. The centre thread of silver allows the toy to be unscrewed to give play on the hand twisted and waxed linen cord. The yo-yo fits into a turned box of Czech beech wood set with a crystal watch glass through which the decoration may be viewed.
5 cm diameter, 3·5 cm wide

Nichola Fletcher
Silver pendant, with inserts of silver tube and rainbow coloured perspex. The perspex has been dyed and its flexibility utilised to snap it into place.
4 cm radius

Fiona J Forder
Silver and leather Bowl
Standard silver, leather (sheepskin)
Research into ancient uses of leather for a thesis revealed a method of forming wet leather over moulds, known as "cuir boulli".
The leather (in this case approx 4 mm thick) was soaked for 24 hours in water, then subsequently pressed over a wooden former and left until almost completely dry. Still on the former a burnisher was used to press down the leather in parts to produce a pattern of flower shapes on the surface of the leather. When the leather has completely dried out it is very rigid and retains its shape permanently (unless subjected to a prolonged soaking). The interior silver bowl was part hand-raised and then spun over the same wooden former.
The silver stand echoes the flower shapes of the leather, it is constructed of many saw-pierced flowers soldered together into a strip, then round into a ring.
7·0 cm diam.

Margaret Shepherd
Portrait Brooch
The portrait brooch depicts a girl sheltering under an ivory umbrella from a cloud-burst as she clutches a flower. The brooch is made of 9 ct yellow gold with details of white gold and red gold. The ivory umbrella is carved in semi-relief and set with a diamond at the apex. Two diamonds are set in the girl's hair as water drops and the flower is in red gold. The face and hands were modelled in wax and then cast into gold using the lost-wax process.
5·7 cm diameter.

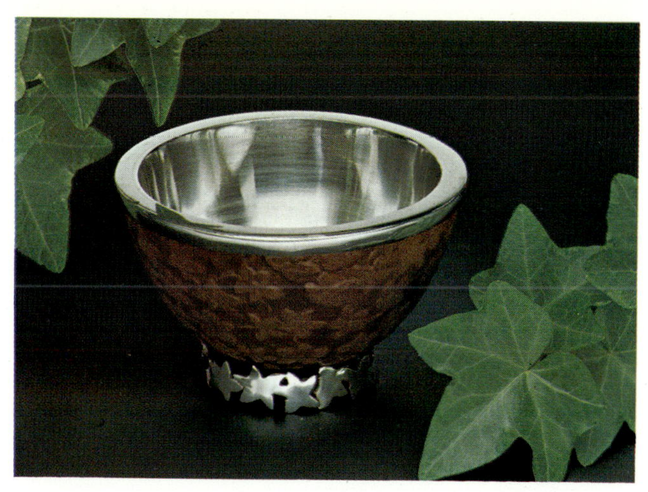

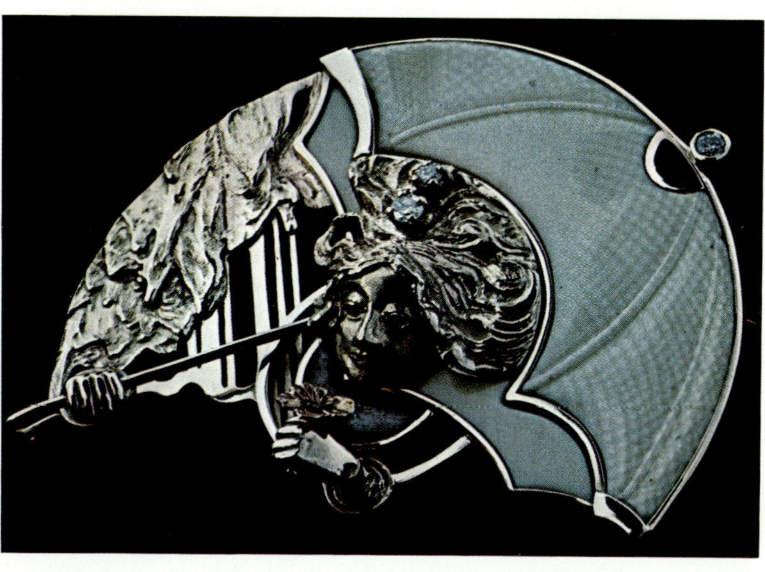

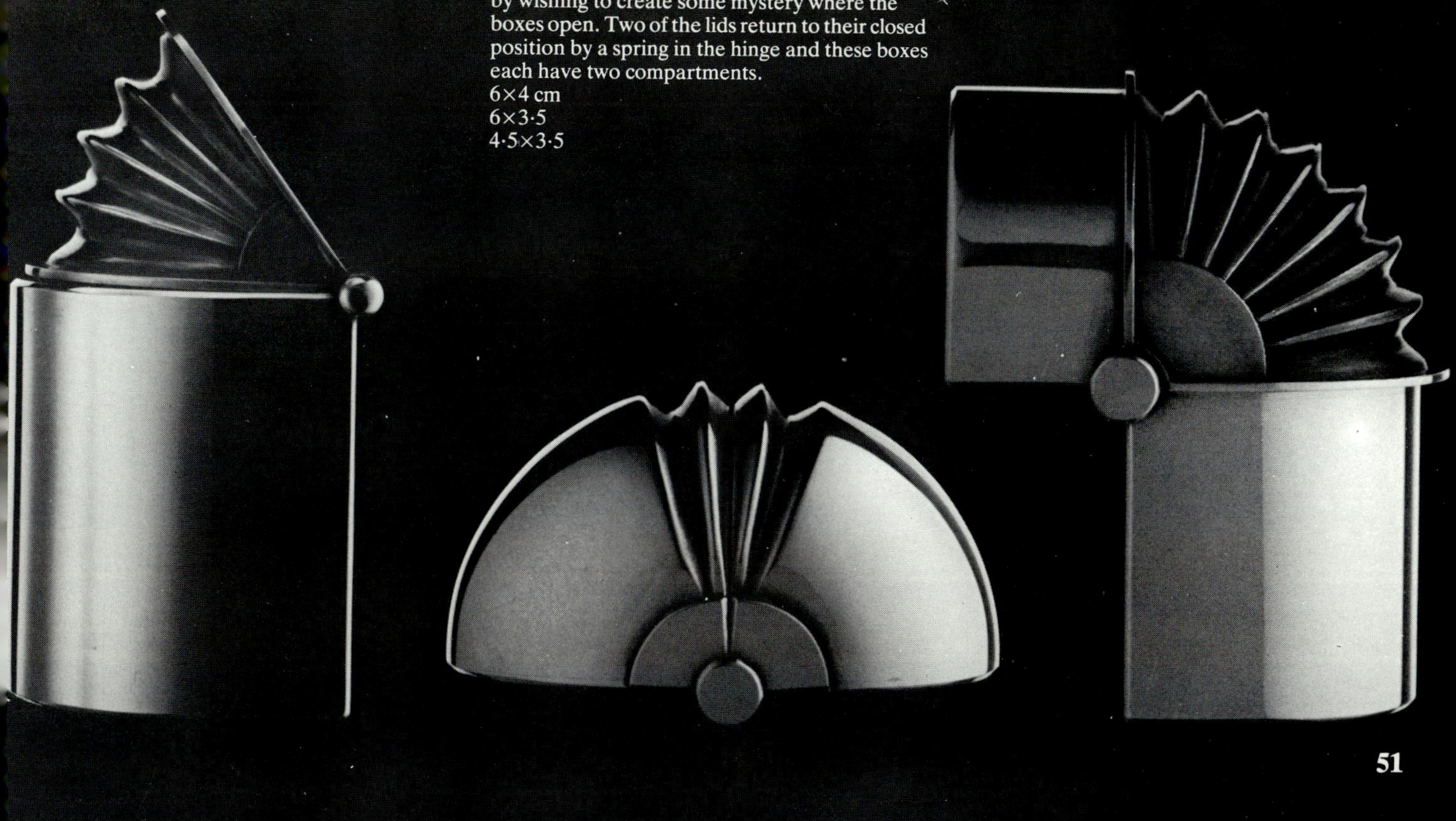

John Creed
Three small boxes standard silver and 9 ct
gold.
These shapes have evolved by the interest in
deformation that occurs when tube is bent, and
by wishing to create some mystery where the
boxes open. Two of the lids return to their closed
position by a spring in the hinge and these boxes
each have two compartments.
6×4 cm
6×3·5
4·5×3·5

Mosaic

Mosaic work is carried out on walls, floors or panels, using regular shaped glass and stone tesserae. Historic mosaic work commands worldwide respect and attention but commercialization of the craft process from the 1890s onwards resulted in a fall in the standard and hence the reputation of modern work.

However, the opportunities provided by the massive post-second World War rebuilding programmes stimulated a revival of interest in the craft, led by Leger in France and Severini in Italy. Today, there are mosaic artist-craftsmen working as far afield as Italy, Holland, France, Belgium, Japan, Nigeria, Australia, Mexico and the USA, their main point of contact being through Lucio Orsini in Venice, who is the major supplier of Venetian smalti (coloured glass).

In Britain, this post-War revival produced the work of craftsmen such as the Unger/Schulze partnership, whose monochromatic work drew students from all over the world, and prompted a return to the traditional direct setting method. The recession in the building industry during the late 1960s resulted in a decline in architectural commissions and the re-organisation of the Art Colleges pruned most of the architecturally related courses. Mosaicists outside the trade had to go it alone, or turn to smaller scale work. At the present time, Jane Muir of Aylesbury and George Garson, head of the Mural Department at Glasgow College of Art, work full time in mosaic while four or five other artists work in partly trade related areas of the craft. Training courses which concentrate on a creative approach to the medium, exploiting its aesthetic qualities of light reflection and absorption, tactile surfaces and monumentality, are run at West Dean College and Glasgow College of Art.

Greater recognition of the craft qualities of mosaic work, the identification of mosaic artists throughout the world and the encouragement of greater co-ordination of their efforts to raise standards of design and workmanship would all help to secure mosaic work the position of respect which it deserves.

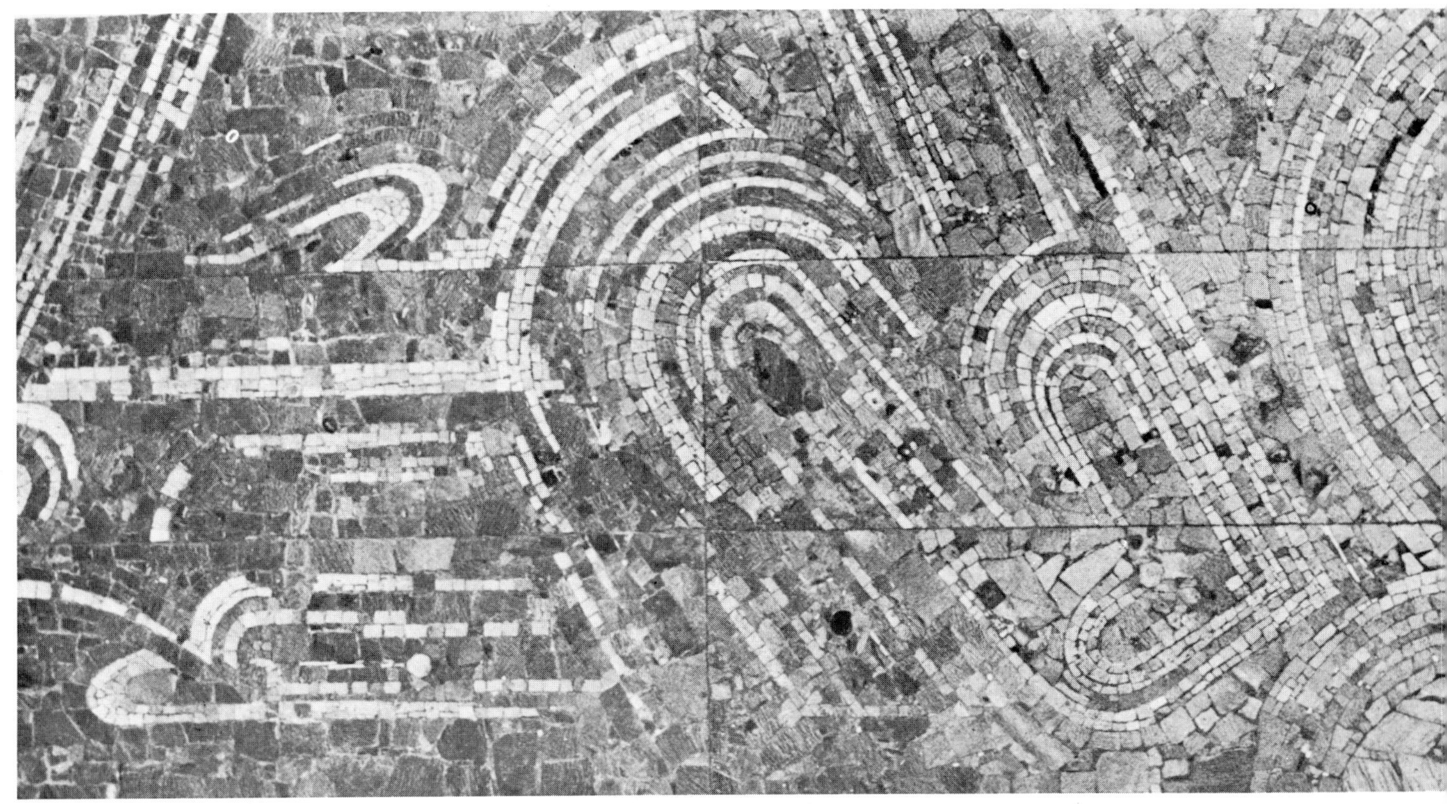

George Garson
Mosaic
This mosaic is mounted in the entrance hall of the
Geology department of Glasgow University.
Over six hundred fossils and minerals are hidden
in it, ranging from trilobites from the cambrian of
Kicking Horse pass, Alberta, to pyrope garnets
from Rajputana, India, gifted in 1890 by the
Maharanah of Oodeypore.
The overall design of the mosaic suggests the
structures found in rocks. It is made of Easdale
slate and sandstones from the Lothians and
Dunbar, all of which were collected on location
by the artist, George Garson, Head of the
department of Murals and Stained Glass at the
Glasgow School of Art. Work was funded by an
anonymous donation increased by gifts from the
British National Oil Corporation and matched by
a grant from the Scottish Arts Council's 'Art for
public areas' scheme. Fossils and minerals were
donated from the Hunterian Museum and the
Geology department's teaching collections.
734×184 cm

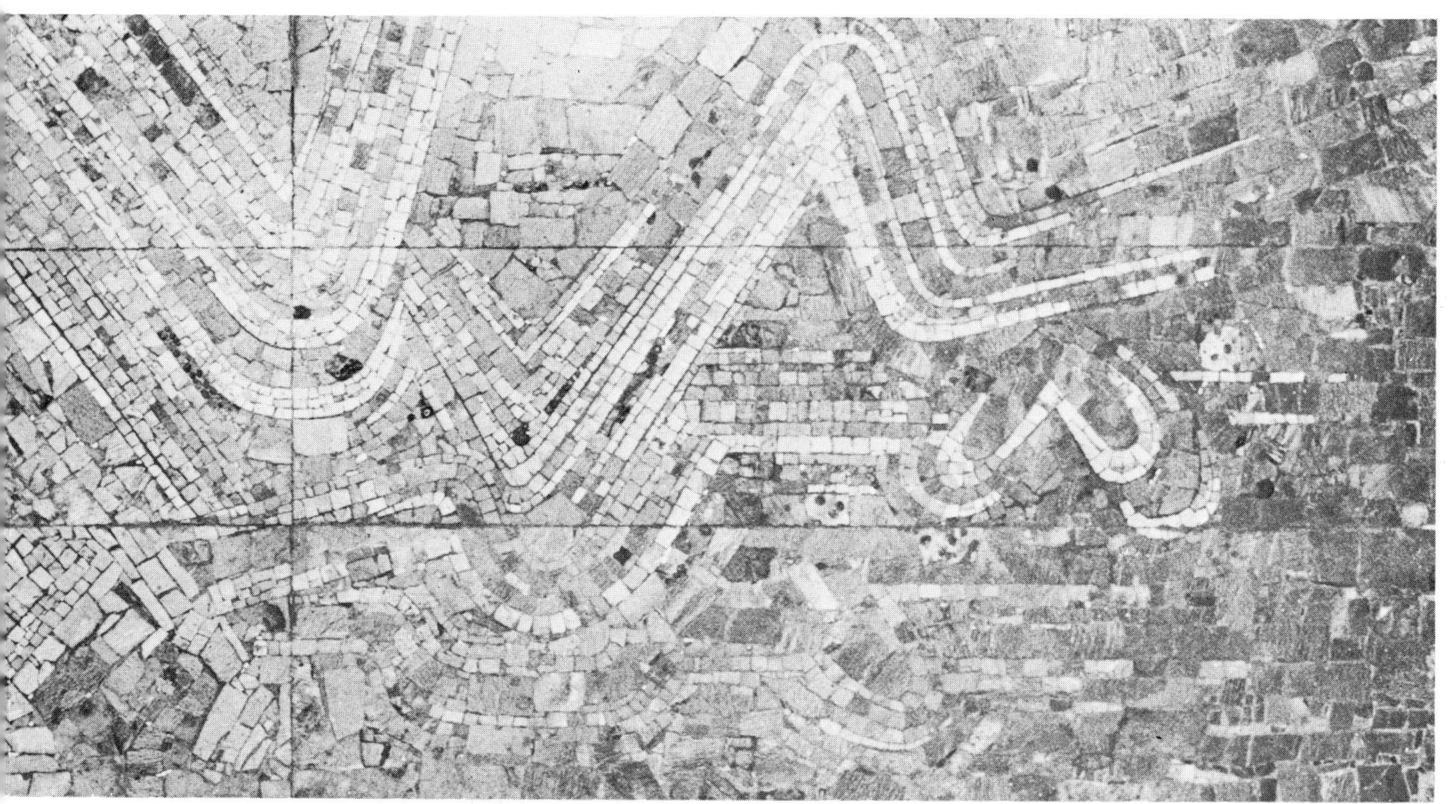

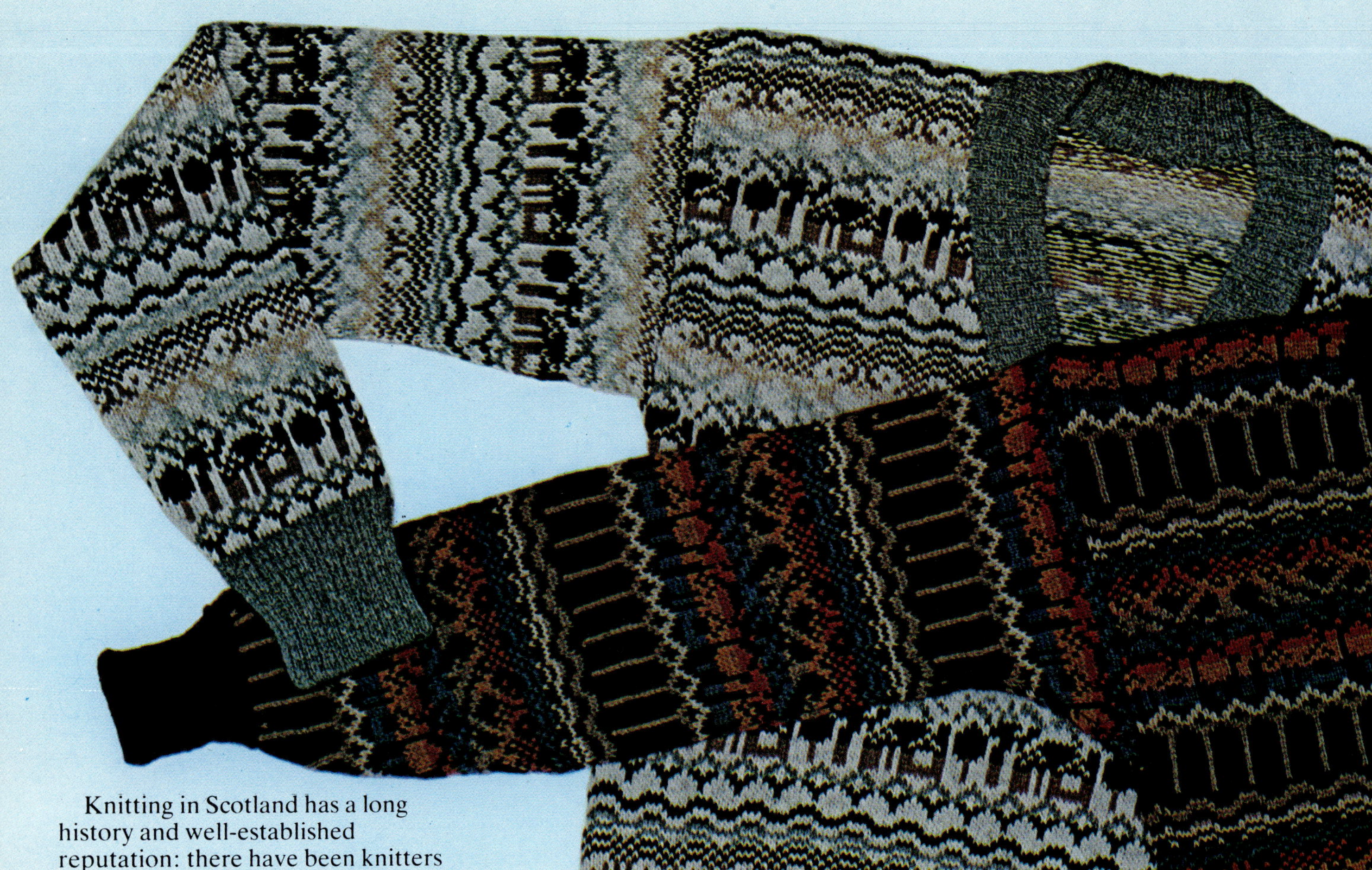

Knitting in Scotland has a long history and well-established reputation: there have been knitters here for at least five hundred years, and Scottish knitwear has been famous for its quality for well over two centuries. Today it is still one of the crafts the visitor most strongly associates with the country.

Knitting is arguably the most versatile and accessible of the textile crafts, since the technique places the minimum of restraints on the designer and requires little in the way of space and equipment. The finished product may be flat or three-dimensional and, at least in handknitting, can be made direct from the yarn without the intermediate stages of cutting and sewing necessary when working with cloth; the stitch and the colour and quality of the yarn can all be varied at any stage. For all this, knitting is the Cinderella of Scottish crafts: it has tended to have a homespun, utilitarian image and only recently have craftsmen began to explore its design potential.

Much of the current interest in knitting stems from the early 1970s when, under the influence of the fashion idustry's pre-occupation with ethnic looks, designers turned to traditional patterns for inspiration. The geometric designs of Fair Isle and Shetland, for instance, were worked in new colour combinations on tank tops and slipovers; similarly, openwork or lace knitting, re-interpreted to modern taste, was incorporated in smocks and shawls. More recently knitwear has been produced, for example by Helen Egbuna, in which narrow bands of geometric patterns are carefully shaded to produce subtle rhythmic effects, while other knitters have developed the pictorial possibilities of the technique.

Handknitting is a living tradition in Scotland, not only for domestic purposes but, particularly in Shetland where the demand for handknitters exceeds supply, as part of the knitwear industry. Knitting by hand, however, is time-consuming and therefore expensive, and for the knitter to receive a just return, the price of a jumper with an all-over pattern is necessarily in the luxury range. Since home knitting machines are now available which can not only produce a wide variety of patterns and textures but have punchcard attachments allowing knitters to programme their own designs, it is not surprising that many craftsmen have chosen to work by machine rather than by hand, enabling them to produce small runs of garments, original in shape and patterns, at prices which are more attractive to the general public.A sadly large proportion of this knitwear is pedestrian in concept or poorly finished, but the best of it is imaginative and extremely wearable.

An example of what can be achieved by machine can be seen in the work of Margaret Hyne, formerly well-known as a weaver. Her range includes blousons and loose sweaters, in which areas of plain colour are enlivened with bands of lace knitting and striped ribs and yokes, skirts and jackets, simply shaped but with richly coloured and textured panels in the sleeves which have an almost sculptural quality and figured waistcoats worked with slightly stylised pastoral landscapes in muted colours.

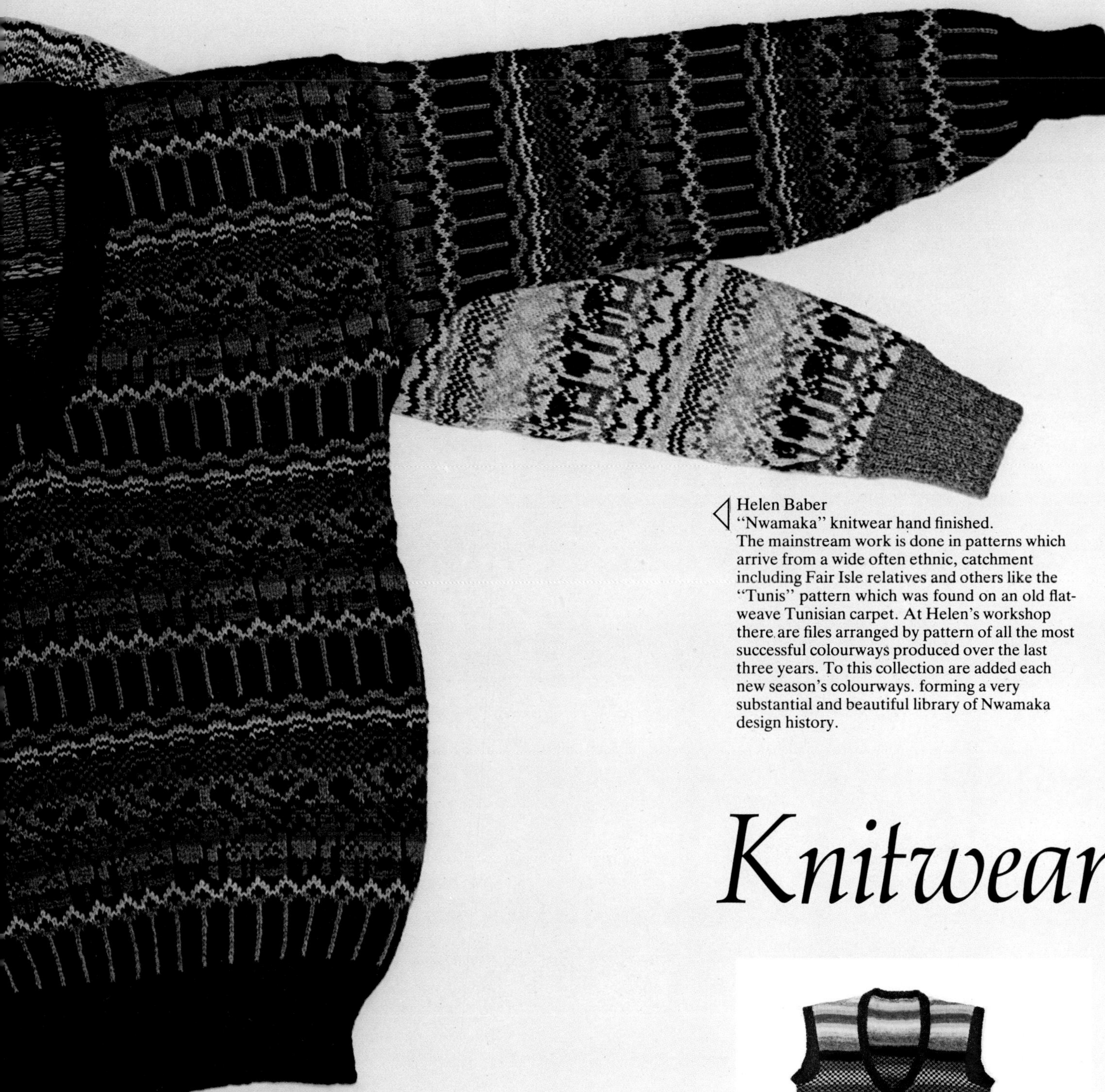

Helen Baber
"Nwamaka" knitwear hand finished.
The mainstream work is done in patterns which arrive from a wide often ethnic, catchment including Fair Isle relatives and others like the "Tunis" pattern which was found on an old flat-weave Tunisian carpet. At Helen's workshop there are files arranged by pattern of all the most successful colourways produced over the last three years. To this collection are added each new season's colourways. forming a very substantial and beautiful library of Nwamaka design history.

Knitwear

Traditionally, knitting has been used in Scotland mainly for the production of clothing: this is still true, although now there is more emphasis on main garments which offer a large expanse of fabric for the designer. For economic reasons, it seems likely that the machine will maintain an important place in the craft, particularly if domestic models can be developed further. Knitting, however, is suitable for purposes other than clothing and it may be that craftsmen will return to hand work in the future to experiment with the textural qualities of knitting and produce hangings or even three - dimensional sculptures.

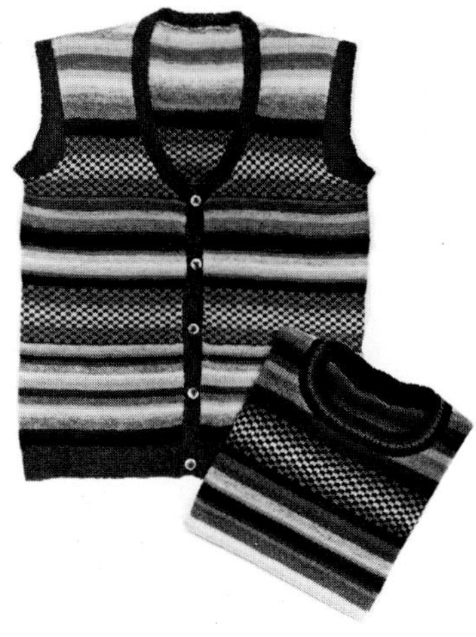

Patricia and Alan Middlehurst
Knitwear
Individually made on hand-operated knitting machines in pure new wool.

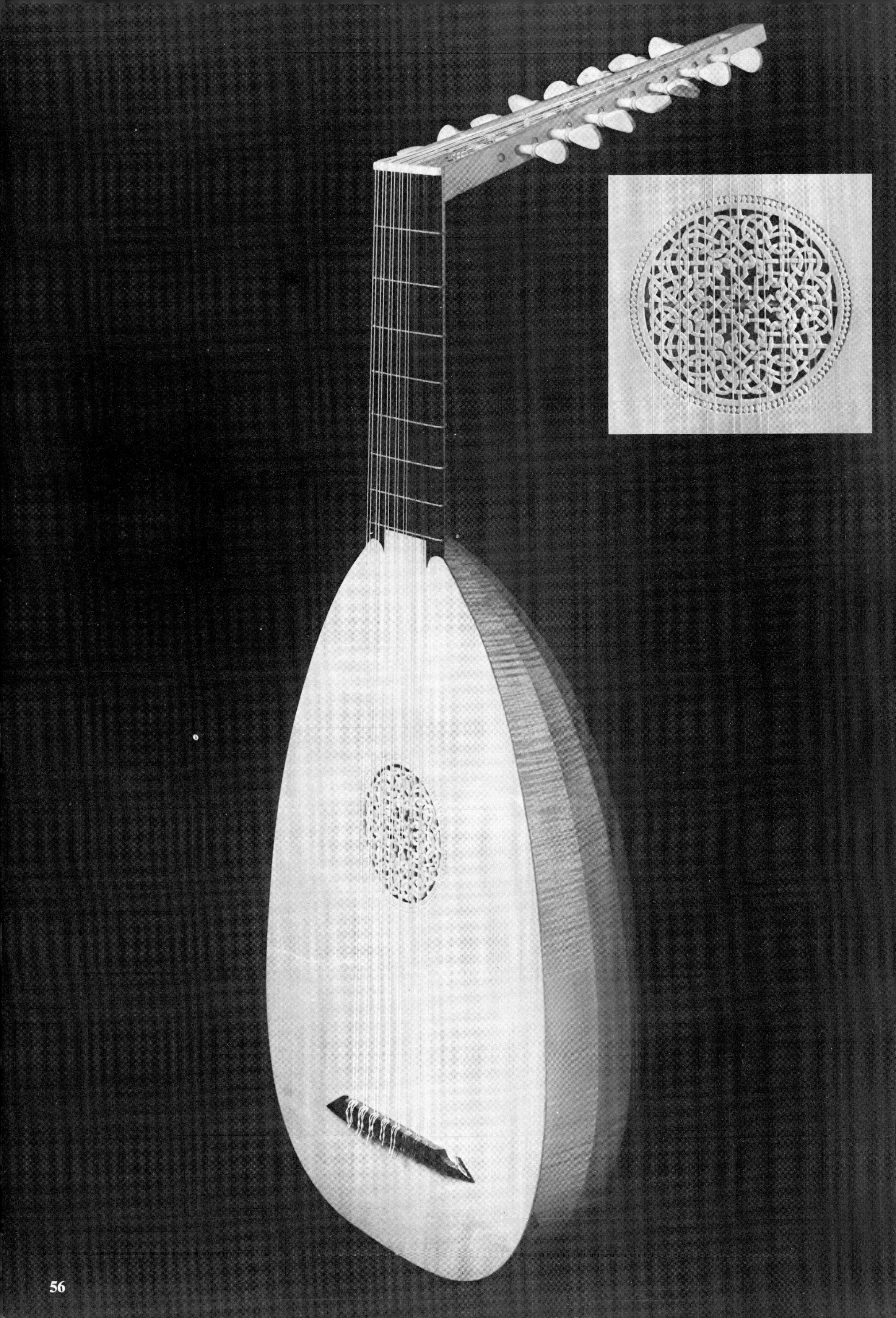

Gordon Thomson

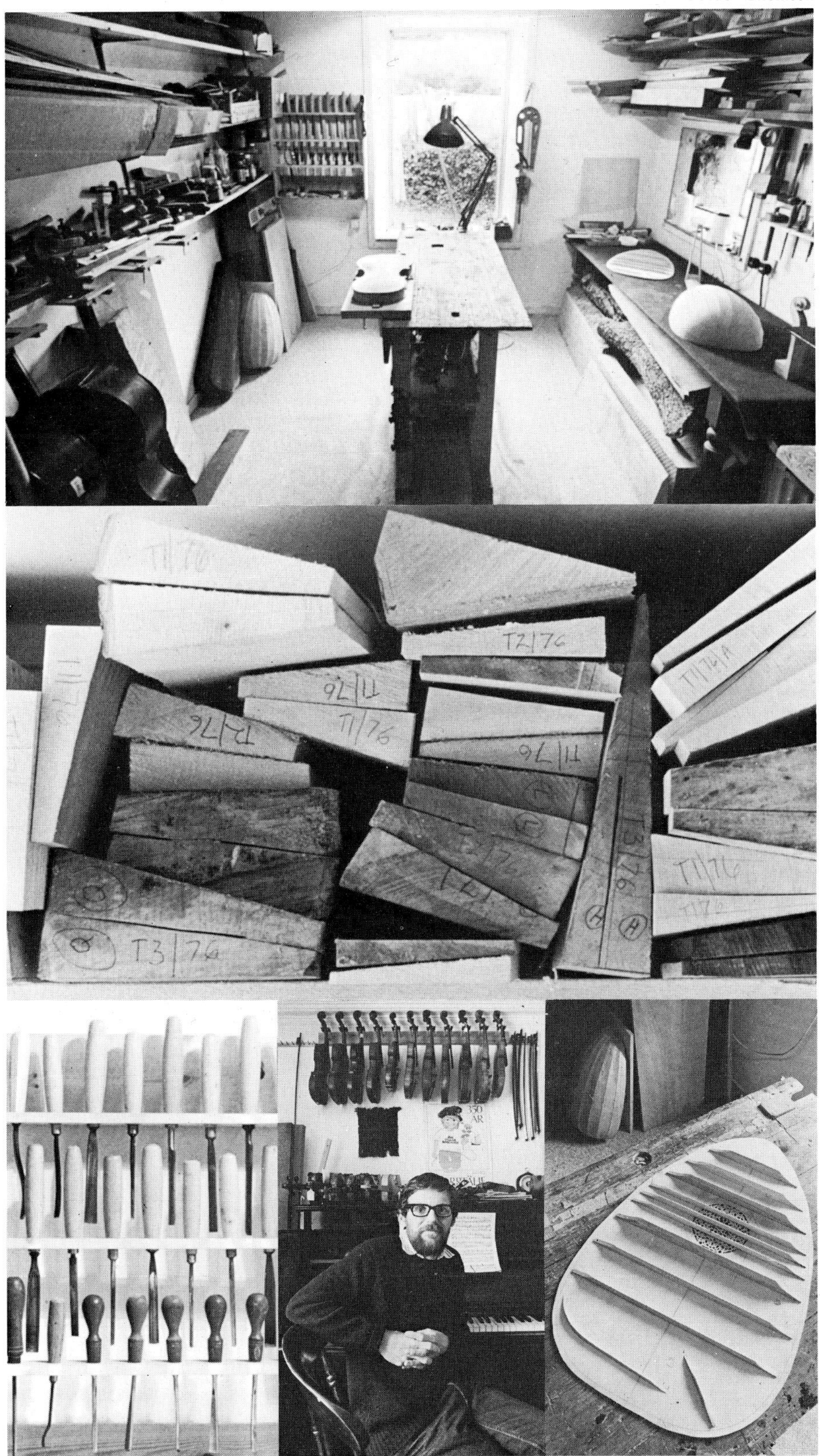

◁ Brian Rattray
lute

The instrument illustrated is an 8 course lute based on one by Magno Dieoffopruchor in the Bordini Museum, Florence. The soundboard is of Swiss Pine, the back neck and peg box of Scottish Sycamore and the fingerboard is of Rosewood. The pegs are of boxwood and the frets are tied gut.

Brian Rattray was born in Inverness in 1938 and has been a keen amateur musician for most of his life.

In the early sixties while working as an Architect in Sweden he started researching into and making renaissance stringed instruments, while at the same time gaining knowledge in general instrument construction as a member of the Scandinavian Violin Makers Society. On returning to Scotland in 1970, he started a part time business as a maker and repairer of stringed instruments and bows and this became his full time occupation in 1978.

Some instruments, particularly electronic, belong to this century; others, particularly those we know in symphony orchestras, were 'improved' in the last; yet others, particularly the percussion batteries of avant-garde composers, belong to other cultures. But the two really crucial elements in most music-making as we know it — the keyboard and the bowed string — are the result of that drive peculiar to Europeans of the Renaissance: the drive to improve what somebody else invented and to do so to a technological and artistic level beyond the dreams of any culture at any other period.

Although this is a very broad view, it does help to explain how it is that in the case of musical instruments 'old' means 'good', copies of old instruments are if properly made 'better' than freely invented instruments of the same kind, and to create musical beauty means to recreate the historical technology and artistry that produced it in the past. Hence the upsurge in making 'old' and reviving 'obsolete' instruments — an upsurge so powerful that, for example, Boston USA reasonably claims to be producing more harpsichords in 1980 than Antwerp (a centre of the old trade) did in 1600. The Bavarian violin-makers would no doubt claim the same.

Thus it is that today Scotland too, in particular the area in and around Edinburgh, has an active cell of such instrument-makers. The lute is originally an Arabic instrument, but it is here that the old craft is being revived; the keyboard was a Greek-Roman invention but it is here that the working with natural materials (especially wood) is now revived to such sophisticated aims that at the end of the day the craftsman finds, as his Renaissance forebear did, wonderfully beautiful sounds being produced. Such sounds themselves inspire good music. Even the 'faults' of historical technologies are imitated: a good harpsichord-maker now goes out of his way to find impure iron strings instead of the brilliant steel easily produced by a modern wire-drawer.

In particular, since 1968 when the University of Edinburgh opened the historical keyboard collection in St Cecilia's Hall and gave shelter to the Galpin Society Collection of string and wind instruments, the fitful instrument-making already found in Scotland has had an impetus and been put on the world map. Its scholars too have, almost unwittingly, created here a centre of work on one of the most basic of all musical details: a history of pitch. The middle C you strike on a piano today did not by any means always produce the same sound or pitch in the past; to know how the great composers heard their music in this respect is a complex subject. Many distinguished results are to be heard here in the field of old-new instruments, and it becomes increasingly unnecessary to look further afield. Let us encourage our craftsmen to expand into all branches of instrument-making!

15 *Musical Instruments*

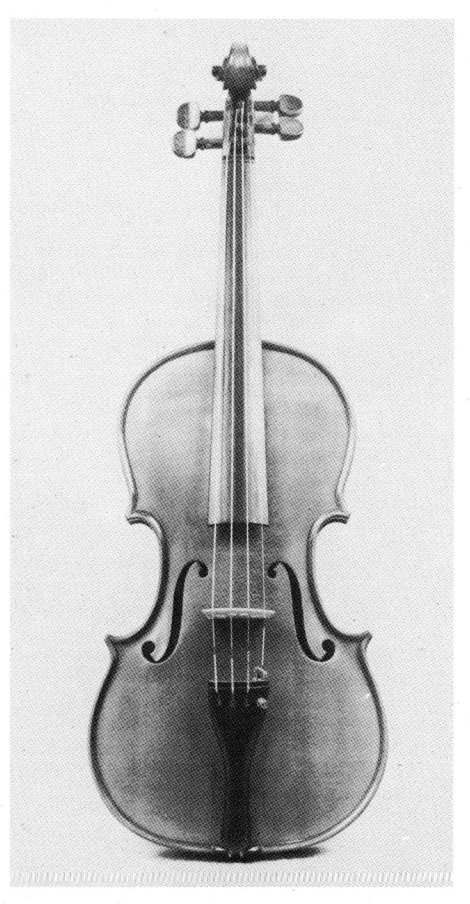

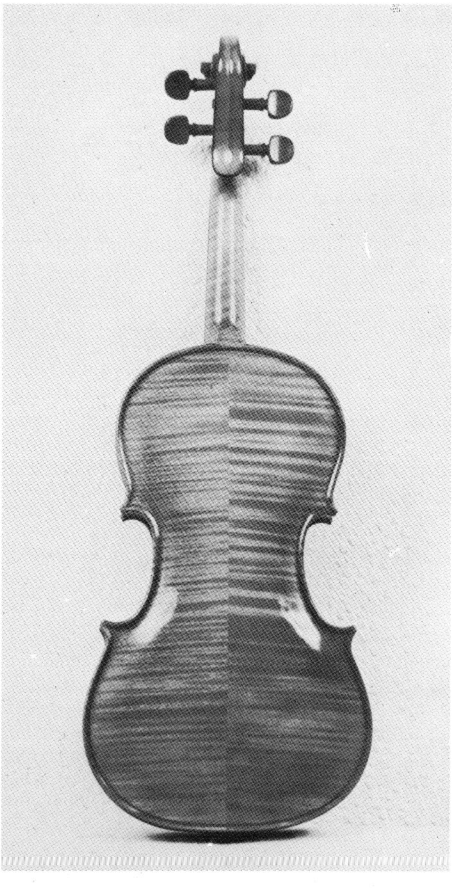

L H Houniet
violin
The entire instrument is handmade, including the purfling which is composed of a "sandwich" of ebony and poplar but excluding the tailpiece, pegs and strings.
The form of the violin is designed by the maker, deeply influenced by the makers of Cremona of the Gold Period (1600–1750).
The front is made of Swiss pine, aged approximately 15 years whereas the back, ribs and scroll are of maple, the back being about 18 years old.
Varnish is my own composition consisting of gums such as: Mastix, Zanzibar Copal and Propolis dissolved in Oils of Terpentine and Spike and alcohol. The colouring is extracted from the medderroot yielding, after due preparation, a deep red.
Great care is taken, during construction, over the thicknessing of the plates resulting in an instrument with pleasing tonal characteristics.

Derick M Sanderson
violin—copy of "The Betts" by Antonius Stradivarius Cremona 1704.

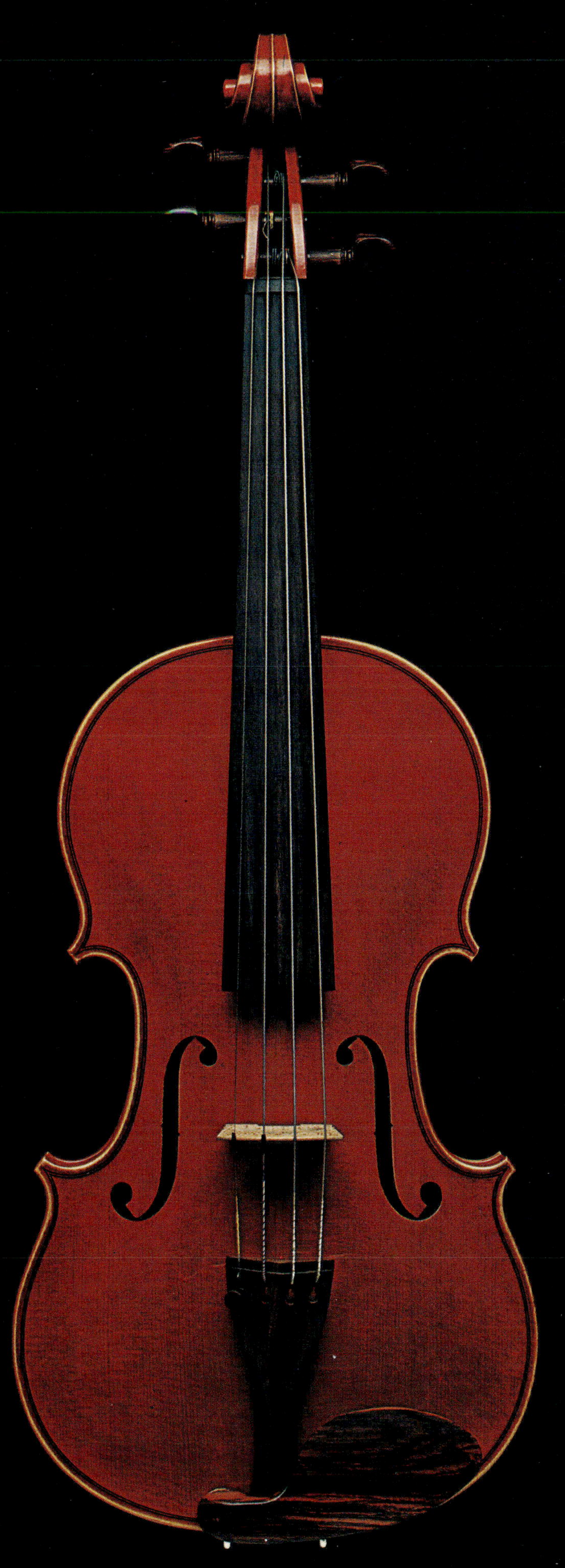

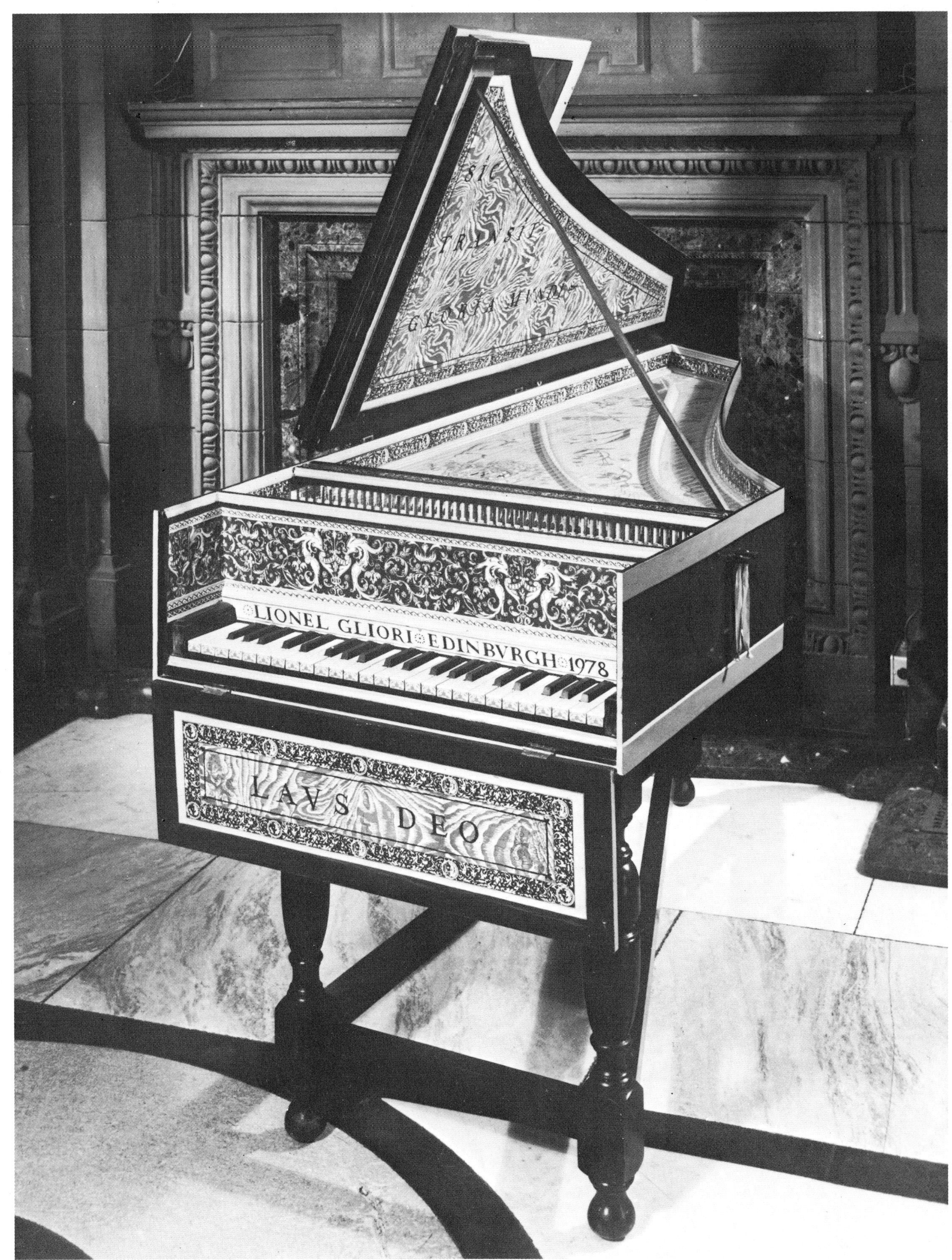

Lionel Gliori
Harpsichord
The harpsichord illustrated is in the possession of
The Royal Scottish Academy of Music and
Drama, and is based on a Ruckers instrument in
The Russell Collection, Edinburgh.

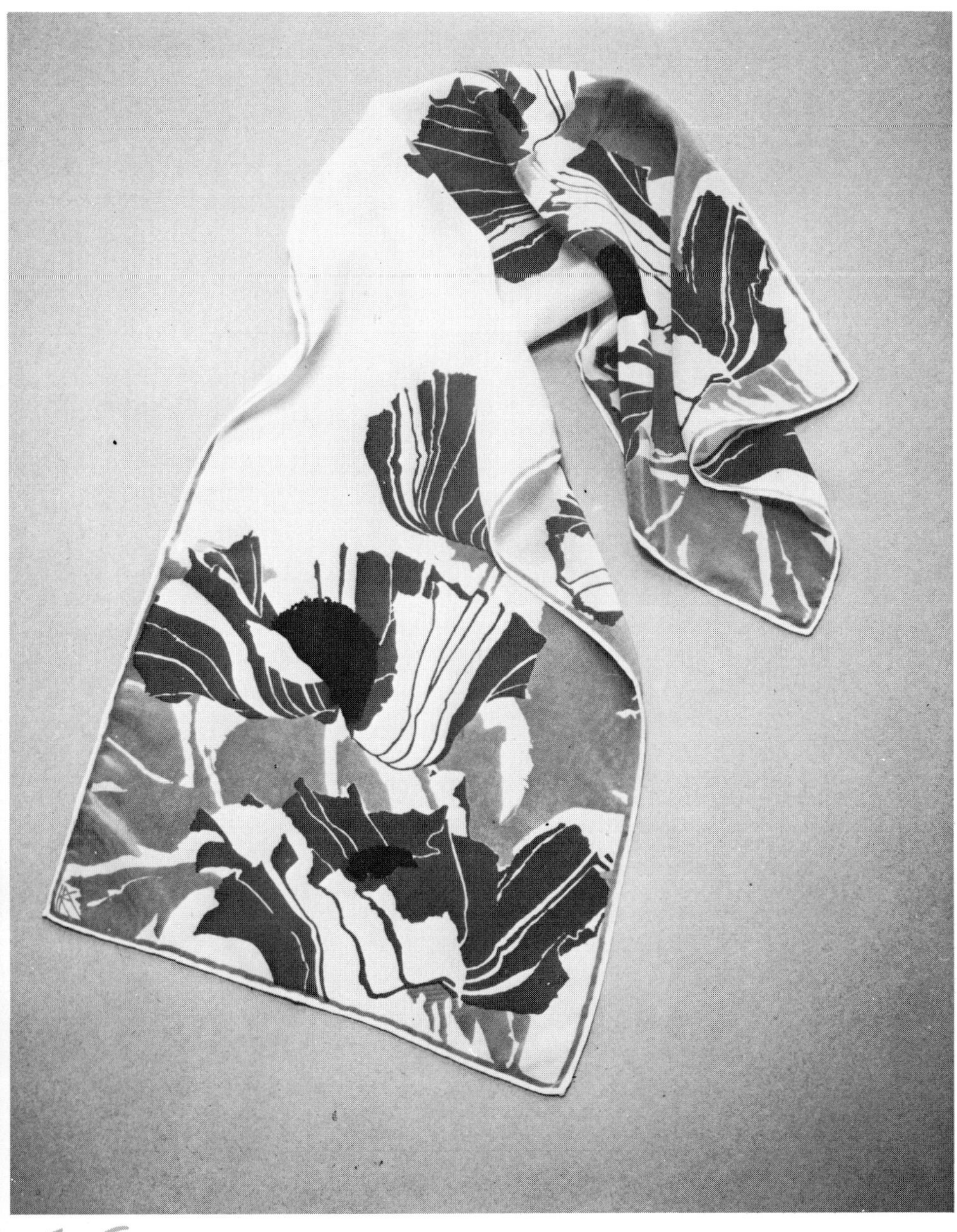

Printed textiles in Scotland today have much to do with tea towels, scarves, aprons and oven gloves. There would appear to be a plentiful supply of these and similar items for both the domestic and tourist markets. While the textile industry in Britain is going through the most severe decline in its history, other areas of the market are being neglected. Cheap imports and reluctance on the part of the manufacturers to buy or implement new designs is causing contraction in the availability of well designed contemporary furnishing and fashion fabrics. In spite of this, exclusive handprinted fashion lengths still appear to be in demand.

Every year many of our best young students leave college and head for London with folios. But selling to the printed textiles industry has always been a buyers' market: many firms do not have a staff of designers but buy new designs only when the sales chart indicates they must. Some of the successful designs so sold earn a lot of money for the manufacturer, but bring little reward to the designer.

A number of young designers now working in Scotland are aware that a reasonable standard of living cannot be made from this kind of free-lance work and are forming co-operative studio and print shops, uniting their talents and skills with designers and craftsmen of other disciplines to produce contract fabrics for fashion buyers and retailers. A new level of interest in block-printing and simple stencil making techniques coupled to the rise in quality of dye stuffs and pigments all contribute to this wish to control the entire process from original design conception to the finished product.

To stem the flow of designers southwards, there is a need for a regional design studio with an integrated team of designers working in Scotland. Such a studio would be capable of producing a strong design identity and of promoting work through the provision of a consultancy for architects, public authorities, retail and design buyers. Lessons can surely be learned from Scandinavia, and nearer at hand, from the Kilkenny Design Workshops in Ireland. If high technology keeps forcing the standard of design to be predictable, well proven and safe because it cannot afford to speculate, perhaps the way to better fabric design and availability lies in the direction of the small unit of designer/producer. It sounds a bit like William Morris: maybe the wheel has gone full circle.

Karen Alliston
Designs are taken from studies of the natural forms. Each different colour area is transferred onto an individual screen by one direct photostencil before printing.
Procion dyes are prepared freshly each day and fixed by steaming. After steaming the scarves are washed, dried and hand rolled (hemming).

16

Printed Textiles

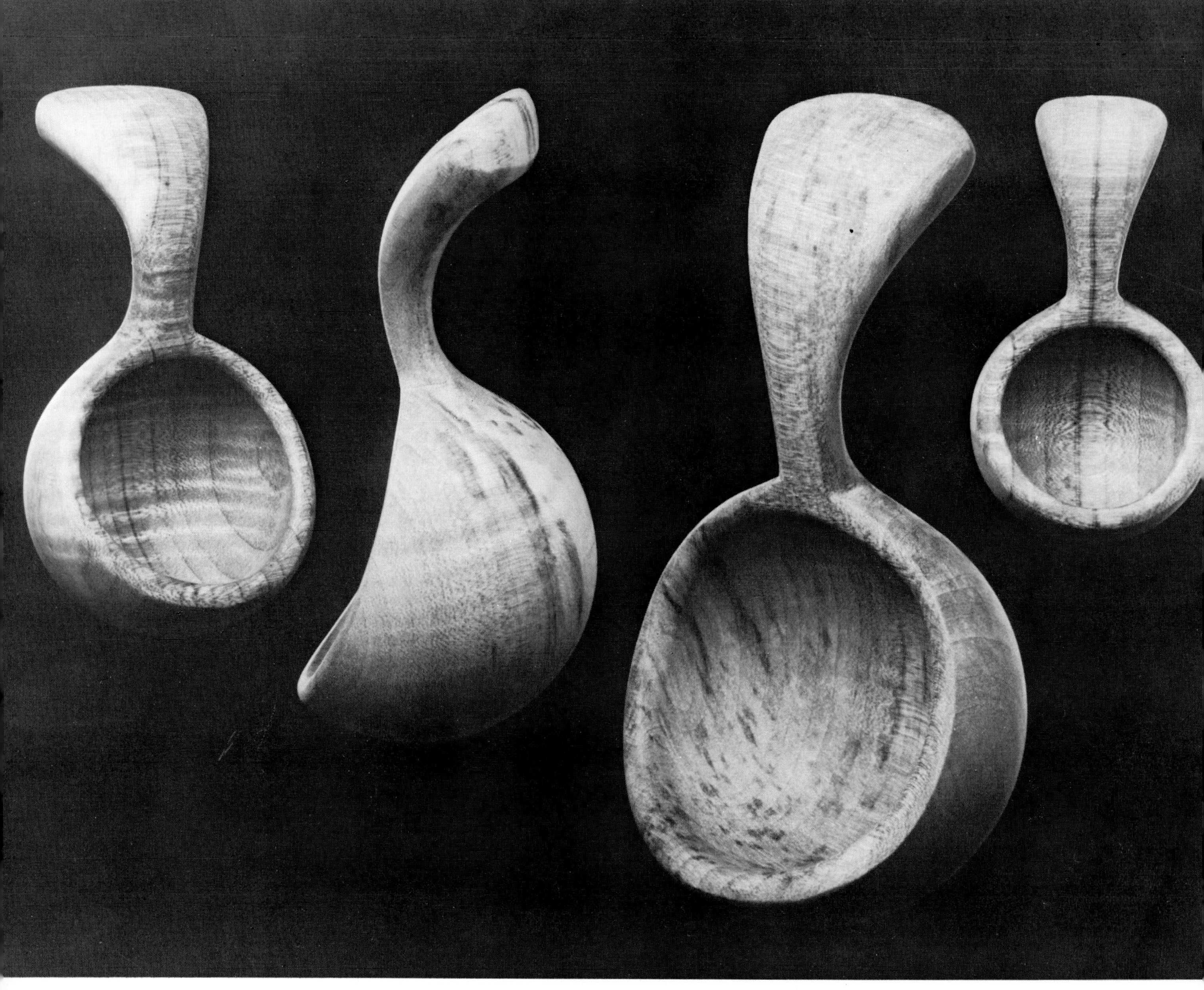

Wood 17

Wood is the most versatile of materials. The fabrication of things in this material and many of its applications are of such simplicity that they require little skill or knowledge. On the other hand wood is a substance of great complexity and its use in modern technology calls for a high degree of scientific study. In contrast to manmade materials which can be processed to exact specifications, wood is a variable, moisture absorbing substance, and its basic structure is by-and-large beyond man's control. Regrettably this fact is over-looked by a great number of wood consumers. Even within individual species there is a high degree of variability, and it is this infinite variety that makes wood such a fascinating material for the craftsman.

The methods employed to work it range from the flint axe to complex machining and it has provided the means for man's development from fire, shelter and tools to paper and plastics. The advent of modern adhesives has allowed an even greater freedom to the designer craftsman.

Perhaps wood's most noticeable feature is its sympathetic nature; its attractiveness to all the human senses and its beauty in growth. What could be more satisfying than to take this beautiful substance, to explore its changing moods and then to accept the age-old challenge with care and deep respect? A great number of craftsmen have done this through time and a smaller number still do.

In contrast to the craftsman's care,

the consumer often exposes this sensitive material to very harsh conditions and many fine pieces of work fall victim to central heating.

The wood craftsman's workshop will almost certainly be cool, with considerable humidity present, and although the moisture content of the wood can be controlled it will always react to changing atmospheres by movement. This movement can be very small and largely accommodated in the design, but on occasions it can be very noticeable. The best counter is to avoid subjecting wooden objects to sudden changes of temperature.

A noble material then, able to inspire the most intricate craftsmanship and yet unsurpassed as the simple stick.

John Thompson
A nest of small ladles in weathered ripple sycamore. The simple uncluttered forms are obtained by a combination of turning and carving techniques. It is possible to detect from certain trunk and bark formations, the trees which give the figured woods required for box, bowl and spoon forms.

John Schofield
Rattles
The rattles are turned in one piece to an original design by John Schofield. The wood is homegrown beech, chosen for closeness of grain, durability, mild taste and lack of splintering characteristics. Special left-hand and right-hand tools are home-made to turn the rings off the central core.

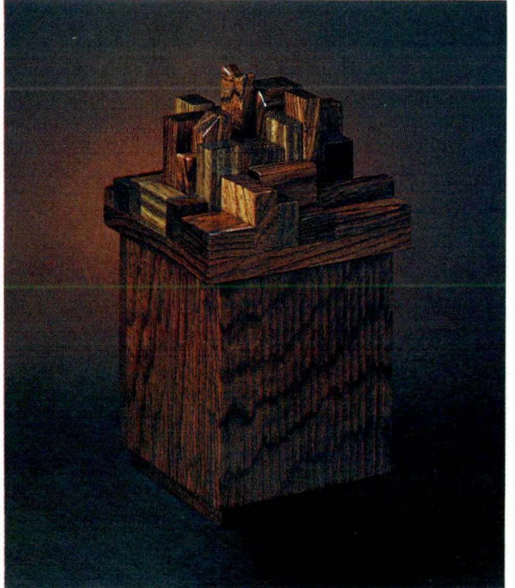

Donald McFall
Hardwood box with decorated lid in Rio rosewood
10×5·5×5·5 cm

M B Weatherhead
Wooden toy boats
The boats are constructed from lime, for the upper parts, and iroko. Each one is hand finished with wax polish.
17·5×7·5 cm

Peter Roy
Hardwood box with tray
This box is made from solid black American walnut. It is finished with a heat and solvent resistant varnish applied in several coats by brush and given a matt appearance by sanding with the finest papers.
32×22 10·5 cm

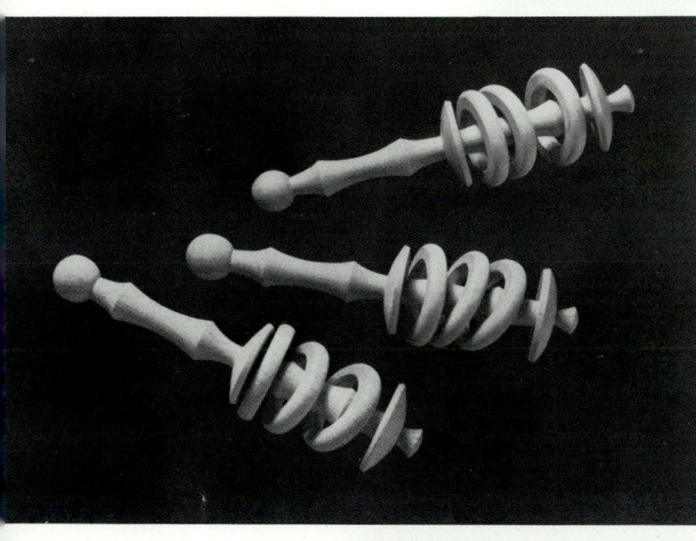

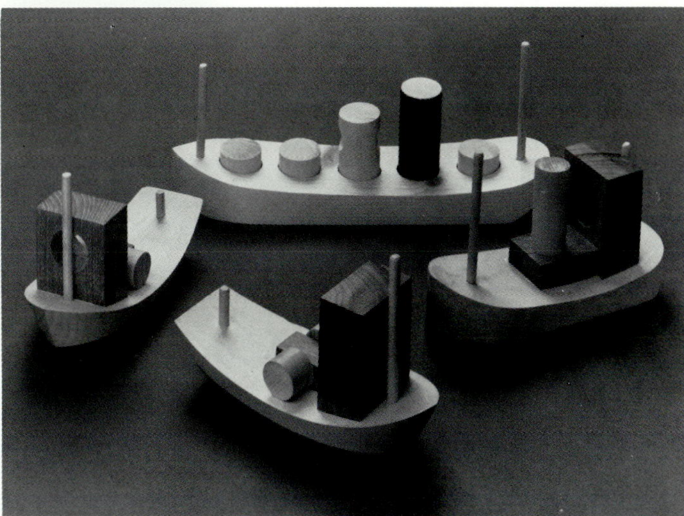

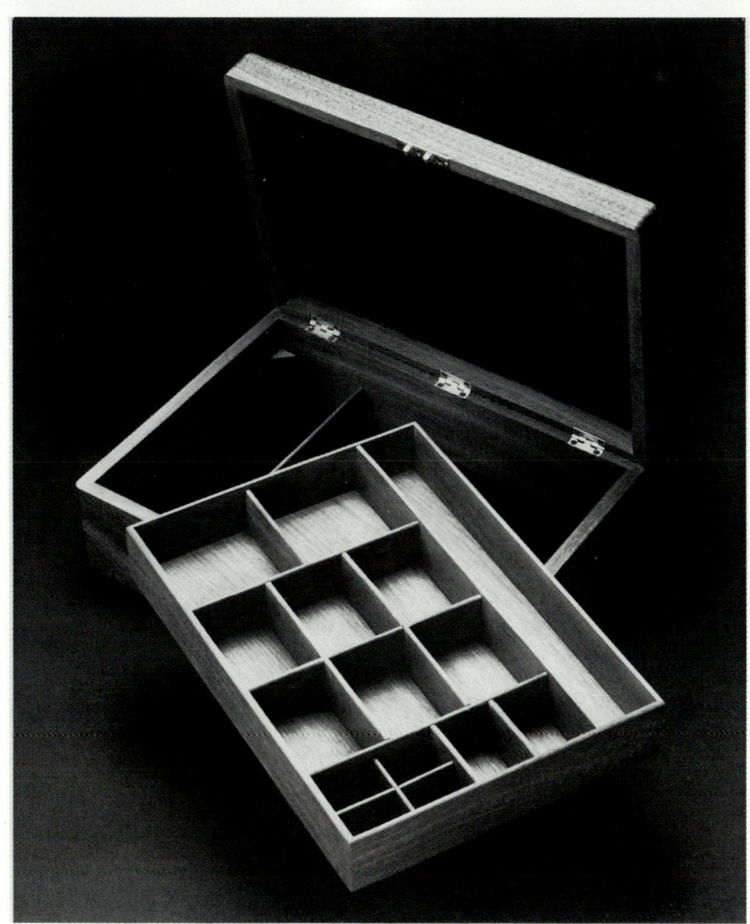

Tapestry

Tapestry has very ancient origins. It is technically the simplest form of weaving possible but it is also, potentially, one of the most sophisticated. In Scotland, however, there is little concrete evidence of any tapestry workshop before the establishment of the Dovecot Studios in 1912 by the Fourth Marquis of Bute.

The Dovecot sprang directly from the Arts and Crafts movement of William Morris and John Ruskin and produces highloom tapestry which is also known as 'arras' or 'gobelin'. Initially the weaving was directed by W G Thomson (author of A History of Tapestry) and two of the master-weavers from Merton Abbey, John Glassbrook and Gordon Berry, both tragically to be killed in the Great War, trained a group of Scottish apprentices who carried on the tradition. After the Second World War, the Dovecot stopped making large historical panels for the many Bute houses. Smaller, more domestic tapestries were produced on a speculative basis from designs by Henry Moore, Graham Sutherland, Stanley Spencer and other leading artists. In 1954 the late John Noble of Ardkinglas and Sir Harry Jefferson Barnes took over the workshop and commissioned work became the order of the day. Since then, under Sax Shaw, Archie Brennan and Fiona Mathison, the Edinburgh Tapestry Co has gone from strength to strength working with many artists of international standing — Eduardo Paolozzi, Harold Cohen, Tom Phillips, Louise Nevelson, David Hockney and Robert Motherwell — translating their work into tapestry rather than merely copying the originals.

There were two other tapestry studios established in the 1950s, one by Ronald Cruikshanks who set up the Golden Targe Studio in Edinburgh, and the other by Gerald Laing, who began Brose Patrick at Conon Bridge in 1969. Unfortunately, both ventures were short-lived.

This is one side of Scottish tapestry. The other is the artist-weaver. All of the Scottish Art Colleges have, at one time or another, taught some tapestry, but only Edinburgh has a totally separate Tapestry Department which was set up by Archie Brennan in 1963. It was largely through Archie Brennan's enthusiasm and expertise that the Scottish Tapestry renascence began. Others too, have done much to encourage the present revival, particularly William Buchanan, while Art Director of the Scottish Arts Council and Revel Oddy whose Textile Arts Association expanded into the Weavers' Workshop. The Scottish Tapestry Artists' Group was set up in 1976 to stimulate and encourage tapestry in its widest sense. They have expanded from the original sixteen members to over thirty at present.

In the world of textile arts today, the mainstream of Scottish tapestry has a most individual style which largely reflects the influence of the Dovecot and undoubtedly owes as great a debt to the philosophy behind medieval tapestry as to any of the modern movements in that the medium is the language which carries the ideas; technique is only a means to an end. The art and craft merge together to produce a completeness where the 'how' becomes unimportant. Recently, like so many other areas of creativity, tapestry has widened its horizons and now overlaps other disciplines, such as sculpture. This is a healthy situation as it represents a growing form rather than something feeding on itself.

Tapestry weavers here have sought to ally themselves with other exponents of the Fine Arts. There are many facets to the medium and therefore many attitudes, and this breeds variety. Individuals pursue what they regard as relevant and important to them personally. Archie Brennan, Maureen Hodge and Fiona Mathison have all represented Britain, on several occasions, in large international exhibitions; Sax Shaw, Maggie Riegler and Fiona Geddes and many others are known well beyond Scotland and so the movement continues outward from its origins, seeking, questioning and arriving at some, perhaps unexpected, but stimulating conclusions.

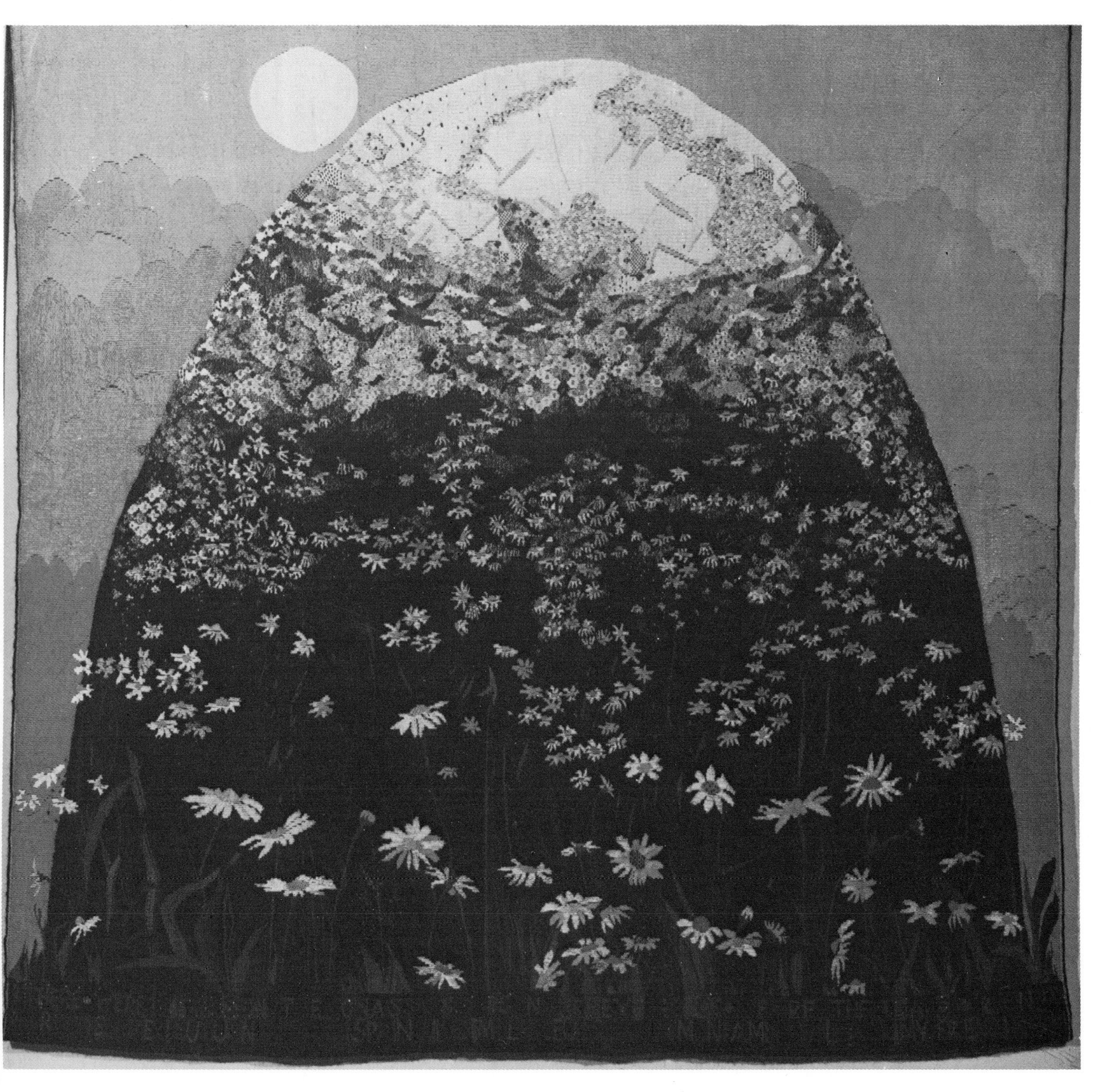

Maureen Hodge
Tapestry "A Hill for my friend".
"There were stars in the grass and stars in our
eyes once, before the tears and the rain. Spring
Summer Autumn Winter Spring, Les mille fleurs
pour mon ami. A Hill for my friend."
176·25×160·6 cm

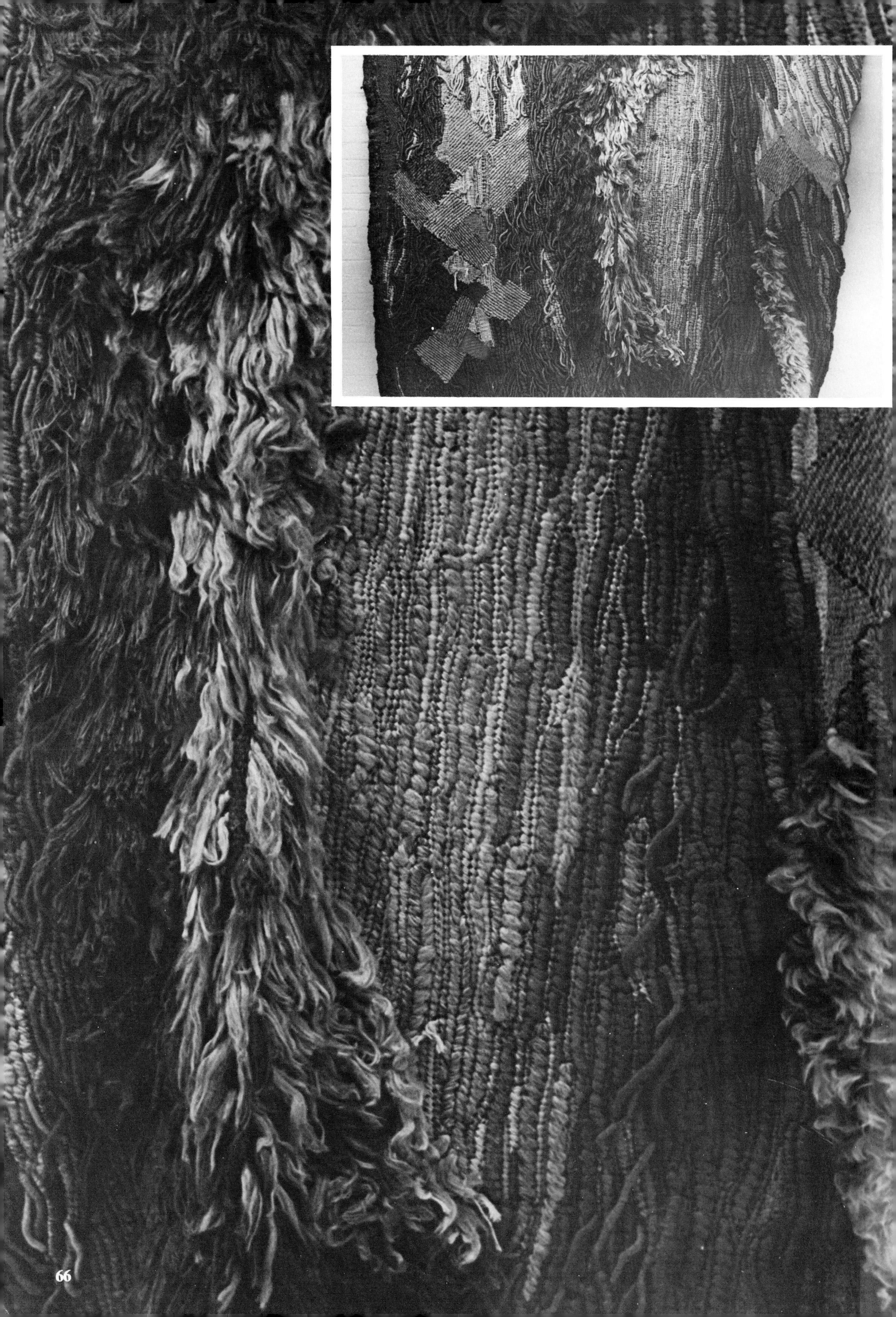

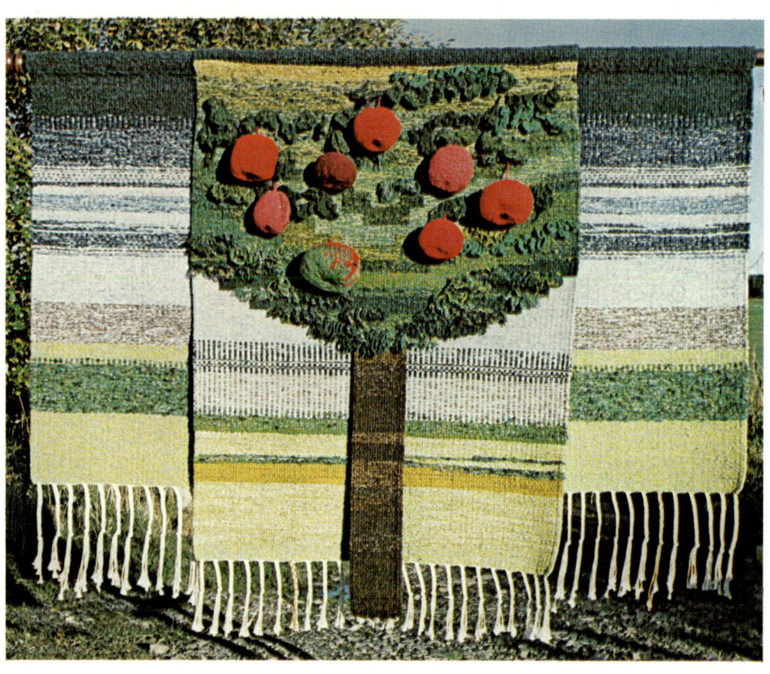

Maggie Riegler
details from a tapestry entitled "Sea Change"
270×225 cm

Dorothy E Urquhart
Skye Boat Tapestry
This tapestry was handwoven on a high warp
loom using natural materials. The warp is of
cowhair and the weft of jute (some hand dyed),
cotton, tarred twine, sisal and hemp rope.
Surface texture is achieved by the use of knotting
techniques and the application of crochet and

inkle bands. The piece was inspired by an
abandoned fishing boat in Kyleakin harbour.
150×60 cm

Kirsty McFarlane
"Red for Danger"
Hanging in three main pieces, two side wings and
an overlapping centre section which has an
addition of a separate woven strip for trunk and
apples which are knitted individually and sewn in
place.
The warp is cotton, the weft is mainly chenille

with a mixture of woollen yarns. The knitting is of
wool, rayon and acrylic yarns. The leafy areas are
partly fringed and knotted in the weaving and
partly sections of crochet with areas of texture,
woven in as necessary. Each apple is stuffed with
terylene wadding.
The assembling of a group of pieces to make one
large area overcomes the limitation of width in
using a floor loom and is a method often used by
this designer.

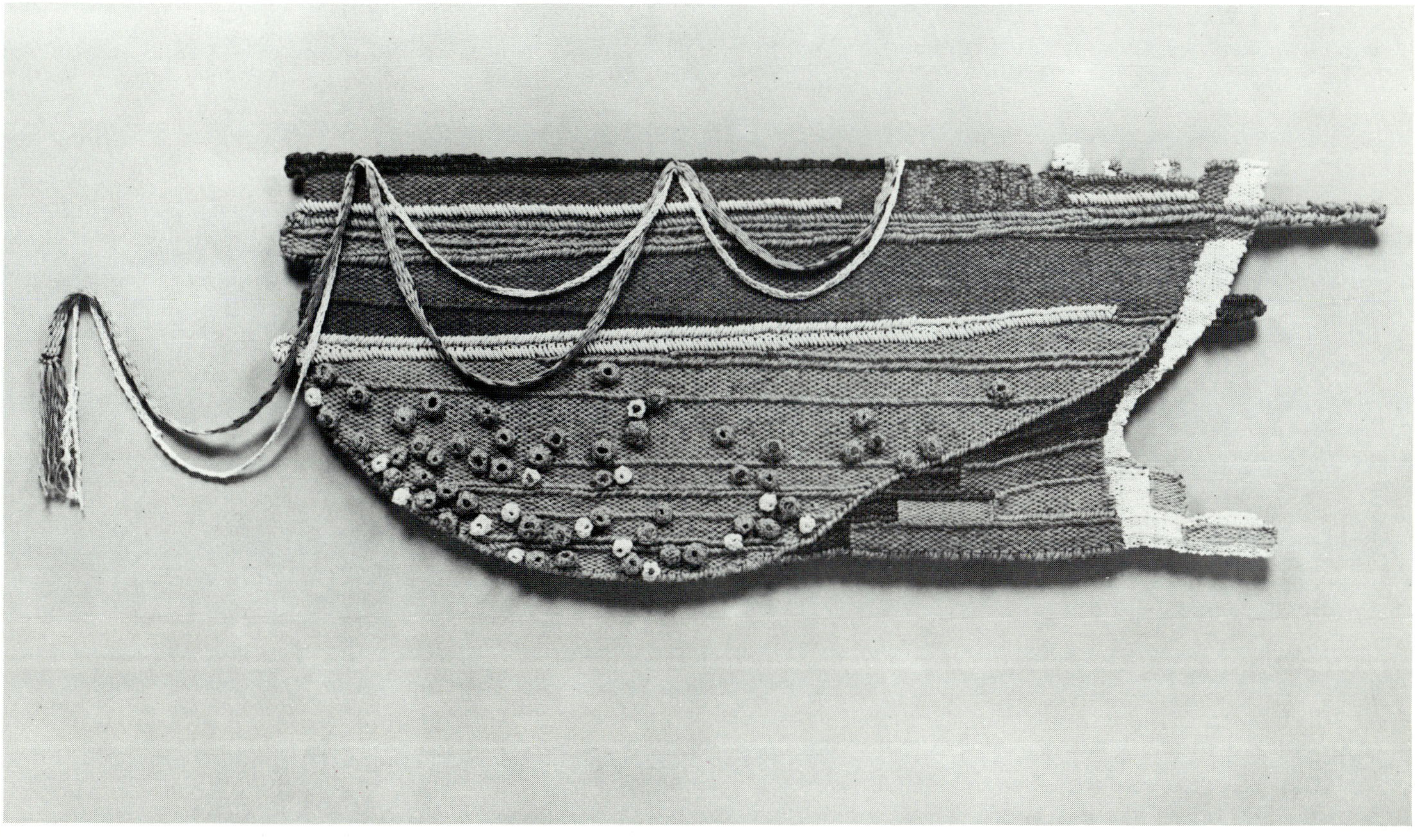

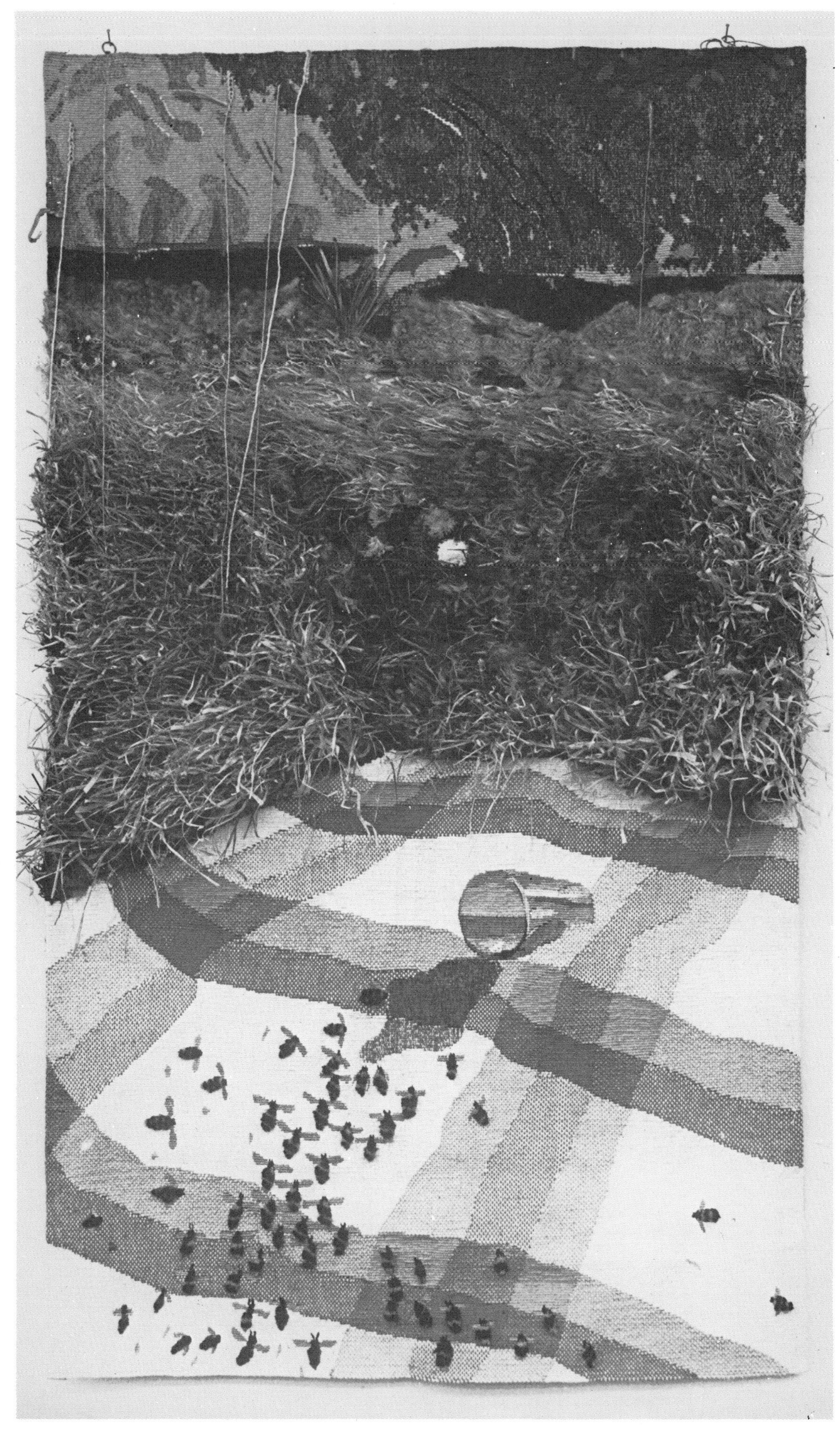

Fiona Mathison
Tapestry "Picnic"
150×90 cm

19 Macramé

Macràme is an Arabic word which is used to describe the craft of knotting and plaiting yarns. When this skill came to Britain from Europe in the seventeenth century, it was considered a completely new invention. Over a thousand years ago, however, the practice of knotting stout twines to make decorative objects was a familiar pastime of the Mediterranean and Arabic peoples.

Macrame has increased in popularity during the past two decades; craftsmen of today may draw inspiration from fine old examples of this art. During long sea voyages, sailors would spend their leisure hours knotting string. Because of its durable quality, macrame-work from previous centuries still exists: the old ships' bell-pulls are proof of excellent workmanship coupled with simplicity in design.

Shortly after the recent revival, thick string, sisal or jute were the most common materials used, but in recent years finer threads have been introduced which have helped to broaden the scope of this medium. By using a greater variety of knots and yarns, beautiful wraps, stoles and purses can be made. Macrame methods are ideally suited to trimming and ornamentation and have been employed for decorating evening dresses with silk thread.

At a purely artistic level, interesting effects have been achieved where knotting is combined with weaving, braiding and fringing; several tapestry weavers in this country have incorporated this skill into their work.

Macrame is a relatively nascent art but it promises limitless opportunities for creative endeavour. Scottish artists have already proved that it can be a versatile and innovative form of expression. Anything from a three dimensional structure made from string or a thick knotted rope object to the finest "lace-like" study can be realised through this ancient craft.

Anne Jackson
Tree Spirit, 1978, macrame, Face, needlepoint tapestry; Tree, 3-ply jute, plain and chemical-dyed.
180 cm × 300 cm

Moira Withers
detail from a wedding coat decorated with fine macrame

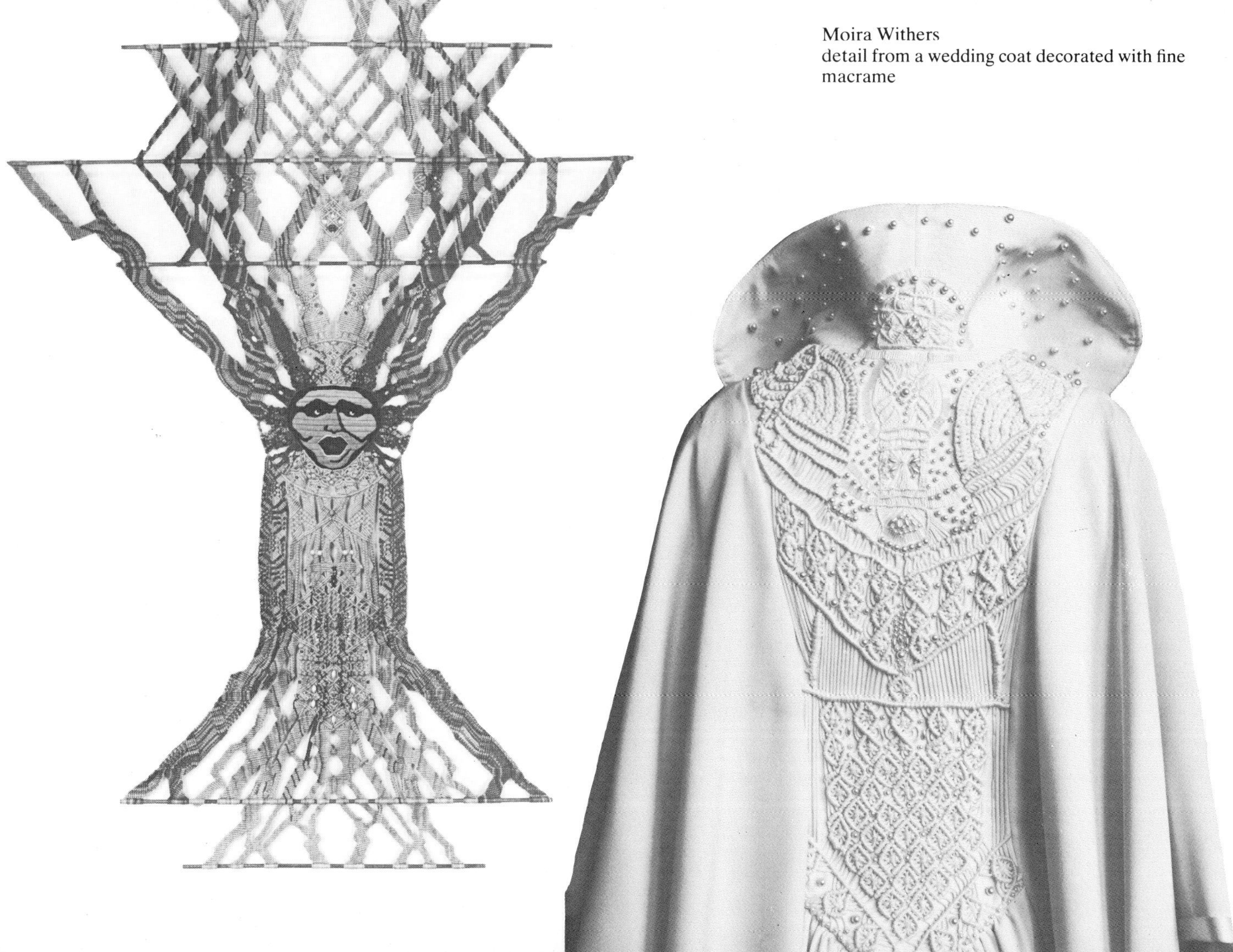

20

Weaving

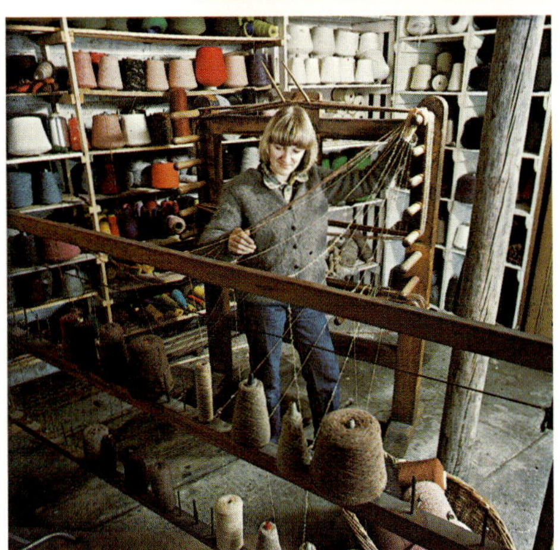

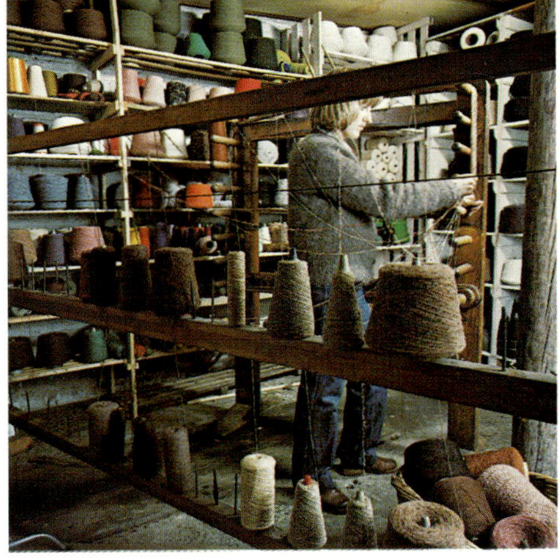

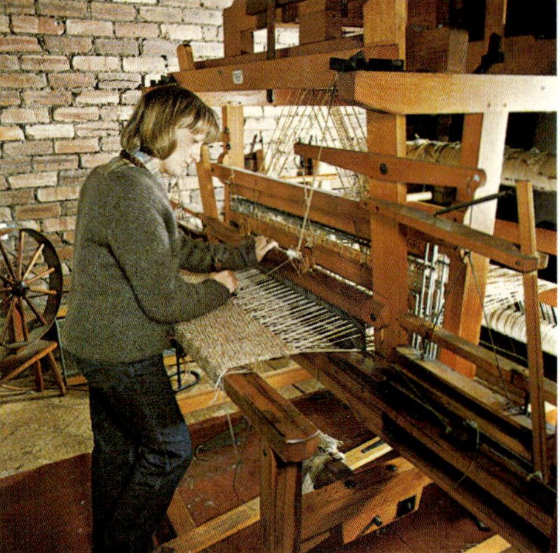

Scotland has a rich tradition of quality handloom weaving. The famous Paisley shawl alone, at the height of its popularity in the 1840's, occupied some 6,000 handlooms in its manufacture. Linen, tweed and blankets were also handmade in large quantities until the advent of the powerloom. Scotland is still known throughout the world for its textile industry; names such as Reid and Taylor, Ballantyne and Bernat Klein are synonymous with quality and excellent workmanship.

Cloth is still designed and woven by hand in Scotland on looms varying from 16 shaft dobbys to small table looms. There is no difference in quality between competent hand and powerwoven fabric. It is in the design field that a handwoven cloth can be superior: mills can no longer afford to weave 10 metres of one design whereas a handweaver can economically design and weave short lengths in very intricate patterns for furnishing or dress cloths.

The availability of yarns in Scotland is excellent. A designer/weaver has on his pallette a wide range of home-grown yarns varying from fine woolen cheviots to heavy Berber carpet yarns in any colour he may wish to use. Jute, linen and man-made yarns are also available. Thus a wide range of textures and designs can be obtained and this is apparent from the handwoven cloth on the market.

Over the past few years, craftsmen weavers in Scotland have not had a successful time. There is an abundance of hobby weavers but few are willing to venture into full-time employment of handweaving, involving as it does hefty expenditure and, as production is slow, high cost per metre. However, the majority of consumers, both resident and tourist, expect mill shop bargains in Scotland and consider handwoven cloth over-priced.

Yet, one cannot put all the blame of a poor sales record on a reluctant market. There are too many 'would be' designers handweaving cloth where the design content is nil, the use of colour unimaginative and where the setting and finishing of the cloth would be unacceptable in the textile industry.

Design education is of vital importance in any field but only a handful of practising weavers have studied textile design at the Scottish College of Textiles or at the Scottish art colleges. The standard of woven design can only improve if more students decide to enter the handweaving business and show by their creativeness and skill that a handwoven cloth does deserve a high reputation.

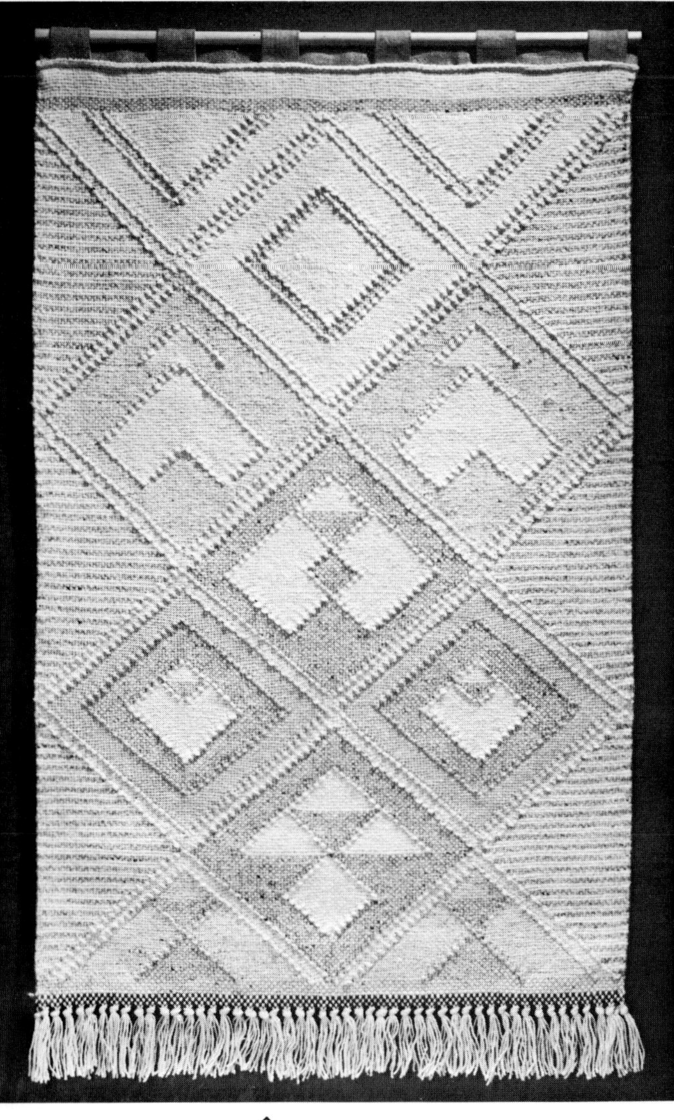

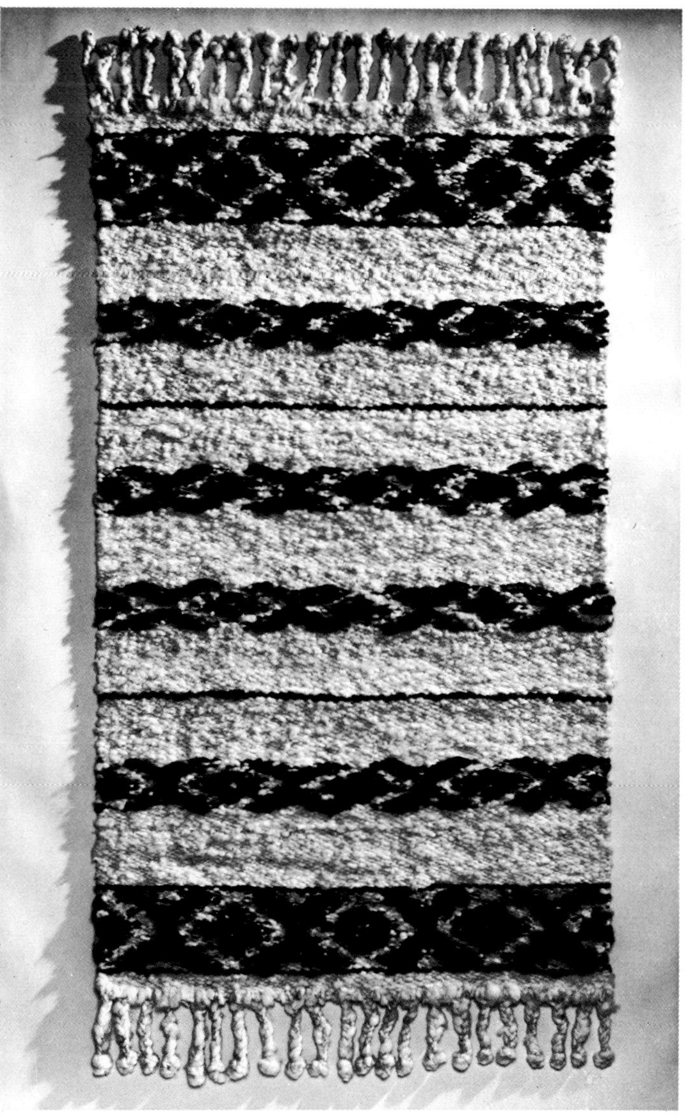

Anna Wiseman
Wall hanging
Woven in a thick soft fabric in which the design
motif is picked out by hand in the weft.
180×150 cm

Anne-Rhona Crichton
Woven textiles

Satya Stead
Rug
The wool has been thickly handspun from white
Scottish Cheviot and brown Shetland mourit
fleece. It was then handwoven into a rug on a
4-heddle, 6 pedal floor loom using a combination
of pattern and plain weaving.
150×80 cm

The Scottish Development Agency
There are an estimated 1400 full time professional crafts enterprises in Scotland employing some 6000 people and producing goods to an annual retail value of about £34 million. This economic factor alone would justify the broad and practical programme of Government support for the crafts. Of equal importance but more difficult to quantify, is the contribution made by the crafts to the country's social and cultural history.

In close co-operation with the Crafts Consultative Committee, the Scottish Development Agency has given new impetus to the crafts schemes and advisory services originated by the Small Industries Council during the period 1966-75. On page 73, the distribution of funds drawn from the CCC-monitored part of the SDA crafts budget is given with a detailed breakdown of the three main grant schemes. In 1975/76 the budget for the CCC's predecessor (Joint Crafts Committee) was £41,997. The CCC's budget for 1980/81 is £128,000 although this is not strictly comparable as the SDA now provides for the Trade Fair and 'Craftwork' under other budgets.

Not only grants
In parallel with the growth of financial support for craftsmen, the Agency has provided a package of advisory services geared to the needs of all small firms coming within its remit. This help is available within the four main areas of Business Management, Technical, Marketing and Information assistance.

Starting up
Business management advice often begins when a craftsman is still at art college or at the earliest stage of a proposal to establish a crafts business. Interpreting a craftsman's objectives and translating them into a viable project involve both the Agency and the individual in a series of discussions covering costing, production, cash flow, sources of finance, book-keeping and legislative requirements. Instruction and specific guidance are introduced as required during visits from the Agency's accountants.

Practical problems
The Agency's staff can also be involved in the development of a project by helping craftsmen to find suitable workshops and advising on the choice and sources of equipment and raw materials. The buildings adviser and industrial engineers will discuss workshop building and layout, the provision of services, production method and control, quality control and the recruiting and training of employees. In addition, craftsmen can receive, in their own workshops, instruction in the techniques of welding and wrought ironwork and in the use, maintenance and repair of specific machinery.

Selling successfully
Marketing is a prime factor in the successful development of a craft business and the Agency has responded strongly in this area. Potential outlets for a specific product can be extracted from records containing over 6000 entries. Finding an agent and negotiating a contract, discussing distribution methods, packaging and advertising are advisory services, supplied not only in the early stages of a business project, but throughout the growth period.

Specialist help is given in exporting techniques but it is customary to test home markets before venturing into overseas selling. First contacts with foreign buyers are often made through participation in trade fairs including 'Scotfair', a craft and giftware show organised annually by the Agency on an all-Scotland basis. The Agency also takes stands at trade shows mounted by commercial firms at venues in the UK and abroad, offering space to firms with adequate production capacity and export potential. Occasionally, small but prestigious displays of high quality craftwork are mounted in response to specific needs and requests, primarily to stimulate consumer interest in fine craftsmanship.

Information bank
For the benefit of trade buyers, a Retail Index providing price lists and illustrations of craftsmen's work is maintained at the Agency's Edinburgh offices. Examples of objects on permanent display relate both to the Retail Index and the Register of all professional craftsmen working in Scotland. For craftsmen, the information bank contains catalogues and lists of sources of supply of equipment, raw materials and packaging. Other references include trade directories and crafts related journals and periodicals.

Promoting through print
Promotion of the crafts through publications is another important area of the Agency's activities. Among the publications produced and issued by the Agency are:

Craftwork a bi-monthly tabloid with an average printing of 14,000 copies, mailed free to craftsmen in Scotland and distributed throughout the UK

A Visitor's Guide to Scottish Craft Workshops a booklet containing paid entries from craftsmen who welcome visitors to their premises

Directory of Scottish Craftsmen a booklet for trade buyers listing craftsmen by their product ranges

Trade Fair Buyer's Guide a catalogue produced for the annual trade fair but used throughout the year as a further guide to crafts products made in quantity

A Guide to Furniture Makers in Scotland an illustrated booklet designed to stimulate the commissioning of handmade furniture

A Directory of Suppliers to Craftsmen Musical Instrument Makers a reference for sources of raw materials used to make musical instruments

Scottish Crafts postcards a series of six images in colour from 'Scottish Crafts Now'

Scottish Crafts Now a glossy publication illustrating examples of the best craftwork made in Scotland during the period 1979–80.

Into the schools and colleges
Future plans include the provision of printed information designed specifically for schools and the public reflecting the Agency's increasing interest within the broad area of crafts education. Lectures to design students in the art colleges have been part of its services for ten years; soon it is hoped to extend to the primary and secondary schools a programme of activity which will include slide packs, travelling exhibitions and demonstrations by professional craftsmen.

Grants to other bodies
Apart from the provision of these advisory services and financial help in the form of grants, the Agency makes a financial contribution to the operational costs of the Scottish Craft Centre (£42,750 in 1979–80; £50,000 in 1980–81) and to Highland Craftpoint (£60,000 in 1979–80; £100,000 in 1980–81). In addition, the Agency is meeting one-third of the building costs for Highland Craftpoint.

Conservation
A new area for Agency support is the setting up of a pilot project to establish a central reference point for information on conservation. Owners of objects, furnishings or buildings in need of conservation will be offered advice on sources of appropriate skills.

Close contact is maintained with museums and other bodies directly involved in conservation activities. A budget figure of £10,000 has been allocated to initiate this project during 1980–81.

Strategy

The extent of Agency support demonstrates a positive involvement with and concern for the needs of businesses falling within a broad definition of the crafts. The pattern and extent of this assistance is under constant review in the light of experience and needs. Whatever form of help is made available, craftsmen themselves must increasingly demonstrate their professionalism, both as a means of justifying continued Government support and ensuring their own survival in a more informed, demanding and competitive market.

21

Grant schemes

Grant Schemes supported from the CCC budget and administered by the Scottish Development Agency.

Crafts Entrants Scheme

The Scheme was originated by the JCC in 1970 and financed from three trust funds. Since its inception, the Scheme has helped 163 craftsmen to establish their businesses in Scotland. The maximum grant, which currently stands at £1560 is paid in monthly instalments over a year to help to offset maintenance and other expenditure.

The annual budget for the Scheme has grown from £3750 in 1972/3 to £22,000 for 1980/81.

Craftsman's Grant Scheme

Grants may be awarded to craftsmen for up to 50% of the costs of an improved programme which is designed to raise their standards and/or volume of production. This is normally applied towards purchase of equipment and workshop renovation. Established in 1973 with a budget figure of £3750, the Scheme has been allocated £8000 for 1980/81. Formerly restricted to craftsmen established for at least two years, the Scheme is under revision to include new craftsmen and to raise the level of grant.

Crafts Training Scheme

To encourage an established and skilled craftsman to take on a trainee for a three-year period, a grant is made towards the wages and other expenses incurred during the first two years of employment. Block release courses are incorporated into the Scheme which was first established by the JCC in 1968. The current budget for the Scheme which attracts EEC support, is £15,000.

Bursary Scheme

Established craftsmen may wish to extend an existing skill or to develop a new one, perhaps in conjunction with a newly acquired piece of equipment or the appearance on the market of new materials. The Agency will help to organise and grant aid short courses to meet specific needs, normally at Scottish art colleges. This scheme is being developed with the colleges to extend the number, length and variety of the courses as well as to encourage a formal link between student and professional craftsmen.

Exhibitions Grant Scheme

Craftsmen planning to exhibit their work individually or collectively may apply for grant assistance towards their costs. These may include promotional material, transport and other expenditure directly associated with an exhibition of fine craftsmanship. The grant may also be applied as a guarantee against loss where the organiser and not the individual is bearing the major share of the costs. The current budget for the Scheme established in 1973, is £2500.

Crafts Fellowship Scheme

Offered on an all-Scotland basis, this Scheme offers two awards annually to allow a craftsman who has been in business for at least five years, to take time from his normal production to undertake a clearly presented research and development project. The value of each award currently stands at £2500. In 1979, recipients were Margaret Shepherd, jeweller, and John Thompson, woodworker. This year, the awards went to two different crafts areas—glass engraving and ceramics. The recipients were Alison Kinnaird and Iain Pirie.

The Scottish Crafts Collection

A budget of £8000 has been allocated during the current year for the purchase of craft objects which will form part of a permanent national collection. The pieces will be available on loan for temporary exhibitions held in Scotland and other parts of the UK. The emphasis is on fine craftsmanship and by keeping the collection on permanent tour, it is hoped that a wider section of the public will have an opportunity to see work of the highest quality which is currently being produced in Scotland.

CRAFTS ENTRANTS SCHEME			CRAFTSMANS GRANT SCHEME			CRAFTS TRAINING SCHEME		
Recipient	Craft	Awarded	Recipient	Craft	Awarded	Recipient	Craft	Trainee
1968						William Taylor	Linen weaving	Alex Wyper
1969						Glen Frame	Jewellery	John Pearce
						Bruce Weir	Metalwork	Douglas Wilkinson
1970-71						John Davey	Pottery	Archie McCall
Robert Dickson	Jewellery	£500				Malcolm Gray	Jewellery	Charles Johnston
1971-72								
Birte Anderson	Jewellery	£500				Barbara Davidson	Pottery	Alisdair Kettles
Norman Cherry	Jewellery	500				Norman Grant	Jewellery	Donald Beaton
Douglas Hogg	Stained glass	500				Malcolm Gray	Jewellery	Stuart Gray
Stewart Johnston	Pottery	500				Gordon Stevens	Jewellery	Nicholas Golbey
Nancy Smillie	Pottery	500				Robert Park	Pottery	Fraser Macrae
Dorothy Urquhart	Tapestry weaving	500						
6		£3000						
1972-73								
Michael & Angela Bass	Jewellery	£500				David Cohen	Pottery	Adrian Gardiner
Andrew Coomber	Jewellery	500				Michael Gill	Jewellery	Kumar Burman-Roy
Graham & Margaret Crimmins	Jewellery	500				Derek Sanderson	Musical inst.	Robert McHugh
John Gilchrist	Jewellery	500						
Lindsay Hamilton	Pottery	500						

Name	Craft	£
Alastair & Kitty Hodgson	Pottery	500
Michael Jordan	Pottery	500
Margaret Shepherd	Jewellery	500
Eric Smith	Jewellery	500
Susan Smith	Pottery	500
Sheena Watson	Batik	500
11		**£5500**

1973-74

Name	Craft	£	Name	Craft	£	Name	Craft	Name
Michael Clarke	Furniture	£500	Norman Cherry	Jewellery	£148	Edin. Tapestry Co.	Tapestry	Gordon Brennan
Graham & Margaret Crimmins *	Jewellery	500	Ron Boyco	Glass	500	A. Porter	Saddlery	Norman Elliot
Nigel Gow	Pottery	500	Alastair Dunn	Pottery	500			
Alastair & Kitty Hodgson *	Pottery	500	Norman Grant	Jewellery	318			
Douglas Hogg *	Stained glass	248	Russel Gurney	Weaving	338			
Margaret Hyne	Weaving	500	Leonard Hassall	Pottery	500			
Edward Iglehart	Glass	500	Selkirk Glass	Glass	312			
Zelda Mowat	Pottery	500	Kags Lane	Weaving	384			
Graham McVitie	Pottery	500	Gerard Lyons	Pottery	135			
Archie Shanks	Silkscreen ptg.	500	Alison Murray	Jewellery	476			
Colin Stevenson	Jewellery	500	Peter Norris	Jewellery	500			
Dorothy Urquhart *	Tapestry weaving	250	John Prince	Jewellery	340			
Peter Walmsley	Wooden toys	500						
13		**£5998**	**12**		**£4451**			

1974-75

Name	Craft	£	Name	Craft	£	Name	Craft	Name
Susan Brittleton	Ceramics	£500	William Edmond/John Dawson	Pottery	£130	Andrew Coomber	Jewellery	Douglas Maxwell
Colin Campbell	Woodturning	600	David Heminsley	Pottery	500	John Davey	Pottery	David MacGregor
Peter Fagan	Cold cast bronze	250	Nigel Hicken	Pottery	437	R. Duncan	Gunsmith	Michael Lingard
Duncan Ferguson	Taxidermy	600	Lambert Houniet	Musical inst. making	500	Ola Gorie	Jewellery	Michael Findlay
Nichola Fletcher	Jewellery	600	Stewart Johnston	Pottery	143	Norman Grant	Jewellery	Andrew Richie
Anne Honeyman	Weaving	600	Pat Laurenson	Pottery	492	Gerard Lyons	Pottery	Kristian Koren
Peter & Sue Kemp	Silk screen printing	600	Charles Levien	Lapidary	500	Eric Smith	Jewellery	Grant Logan
Zelda Mowat *	Pottery	600	Anne Lightwood	Pottery	300			
Archie McCall	Pottery	500	Roy Matthew	Wrought iron	478			
Margaret Oliver	Pottery	500	Irene Morton	Pottery	252			
Andy Priestman	Pottery	600	Peter Marroney	Lapidary	422			
Alan Ross	Wooden Toys	500						
Eric Smith *	Jewellery	250						
Peter Walmsley *	Wooden toys	500						
14		**£7200**	**11**		**£4154**			

1975-76

Name	Craft	£	Name	Craft	£	Name	Craft	Name
Kenneth Anderson	Furniture	£500	Len Ashton	Wooden toys, woodturning	£343	Alistair Hodgson	Pottery	Alex Forrester
William Brown & Ian Pirie	Pottery	600	Bemersyde Pottery	Pottery	332	Patricia Hassall	Pottery	Hope Mason
Constance Chase	Weaving	600	Susan Brittleton	Pottery	500	David Heminsley	Pottery	Susan Campbell
Michael Clarke *	Furniture	300	Bryan & Doris Green	Leather collage	477	Scott Myles	Woodturning	William Peat
Anne Rhona Crichton	Weaving	600	Ian Hird	Pottery	500	John Gilchrist	Jewellery	Brian Aitken
Hugh Falconer	Pottery	600	Stewart Johnston	Pottery	108			
Duncan Ferguson *	Taxidermy	300	Donald McGarva	Furniture	495			
Earl Hart	Leather	750	John Urwin	Woodturning	334			
Peter & Sue Kemp *	Silk screen printing	400	Stanley Whyte	Woodturning	456			
Ian Ketchin	Woodturning	600						
Robert Lye	Reproduction firearms	400						
Peter Machel	Weaving	600						
Alan & Patricia Middlehurst	Knitting	600						
Vera Macdonald	Knitting	150						
Margaret Oliver *	Pottery	300						
Andy Priestman *	Pottery	300						
John Schofield	Furniture	600						
Bert Simpson	Pottery	600						
Tim Stead	Furniture	600						
Tim Stimson	Pottery	200						
Jane Stunt	Tapestry weaving	300						
Jack Torbet	Woodturning	750						
Michael Williamson	Pottery	600						
Annna Wiseman	Weaving	600						
24		**£11850**	**9**		**£3545**			

1976-77

Name	Craft	£	Name	Craft	£	Name	Craft	Name
Karen Allison	Silk screen printing	£375	Barbara Davidson	Pottery	£500	Border Fine Art	Figurine Modelling	Mairi Laing
Jack Cunningham	Jewellery	750	Mark Jones	Resins	268	Beryl Tittensor	Calligraphy	Margaret Tittensor
Marjory Fernie	Weaving	750	Anthony Mobbs	Jewellery	500	Ola Gorie	Jewellery	Kenneth McConnachie
Chris Hamilton	Jewellery	750	Charles Munro	Woodturning	258	Norman Cherry	Jewellery	Alison Purves
Marjory Heminsley	Knitting	500	Andrew Priestman	Pottery	336			
Joan Hough/Elizabeth Blacker	Weaving	375	Russel Pursey	Silk screen printing	500			
Ian Leishman	Knitting	400						
Alan & Patricia Middlehurst *	Knitting	750						
Dierdre Minogue	knitting	250						
Denys Mitchell	Wrought iron	500						
Lynn Moffat	Jewellery	750						
Sue Murray	Glass	750						
Ian & Jennifer Macrae	Pottery	750						
Jennifer Rolland	Embroidery/weaving	375						
John Schofield *	Furniture making	400						

 *Denotes further grant

Name	Craft	Amount		Name	Craft	Amount
Sue & Tony Simpson	Leather	750		George Shanks	Pottery	500
Tim Stead *	Furniture	400		Nancy Smillie	Pottery	500
Joan Stevenson/Anita Pate	Glass	500		William Stewart	Jewellery	337
Kathleen Thomson	Jewellery	750				
Michael Williamson *	Pottery	250				
20		**£11075**	**9**			**£3699**

1977-78

Name	Craft	Amount
Karen Allison *	Silk screen printing	£396
Laura Brittain	Knitting	480
Jennifer Butler	Weaving	762
Irma Demianczuk	Pottery	381
Bridget Drakeford	Pottery	762
Helen Egbuna	Knitting	960
Peter Fishley Holland	Pottery	400
Anne Franchi	Jewellery	378
Donald Fraser	Weaving	380
Anne Clare Graham	Jewellery	762
Nigel Johnson	Pottery	774
Knockando Wood Mill	Weaving	500
Ian Leishman *	Knitting	396
D. Menzies	Knitting	762
Mary McGregor	Pottery	960
Robin McHugh	Musical instruments	960
William McNamara	Pottery	500
Jeremy Norman	Woodturning	960
Jennifer Pettigrew	Batik	450
Raymond Plazalski	Pottery	500
Christine Rushton	Knitting	762
Calum Strathie	Pottery	762
Robert Taylor	Wooden toys	381
Jack Torbet *	Woodturning	300
Colin Walker	Pottery	500
25		**£15128**

Name	Craft	Amount
Michael Burton/Marlyn Abbey	Leather	£400
Ian Clark	Woodcarving	494
John Davey	Pottery	351
Peter Fagan	Cold cast bronze	500
David Harkison	Jewellery	500
Earl Hart	Leather	500
Peter & Sue Kemp	Silk screen ptg.	500
Joan Lawson	Jewellery	500
Thomas Lochhead	Pottery	500
Peter Machel	Weaving	127
Zelda Mowat	Pottery	175
Andrew Strathie	Jewellery	182
Charles Wilson	Jewellery	500
13		**£5229**

Name	Craft	Name
Joe Finch	Pottery	Stephen Smart
John Prince	Jewellery	Nicola Stronach
Tim Stead	Furniture	Ronald Lee
Donald Swan	Pottery	John Swan
Bryan Green	Collage	Morag Aitchison

1978-79

Name	Craft	Amount
Janet Adam	Pottery	£573
Anne Clare Graham *	Jewellery	500
Chris Holmes	Furniture	1146
David Kaplan/Daryl Hinz	Glass	1146
Maggie Ledwith	Weaving	720
Rachel Mackie	Jewellery	1146
Heather Milligan	Silk screen printing	1146
Mary McGregor *	Pottery	500
Shirley Pinder	Weaving	1146
Wendy Rae/Jennifer McLean	Jewellery	1146
Brian Rattray	Musical instruments	1146
Graham Stewart	Jewellery	1146
Bruce Walford/Fergus Stewart	Pottery	1146
Alex Walgate	Pottery	540
Susan Webster	Jewellery	1146
15		**£14293**

Name	Craft	Amount
Karen Alliston	Silk screen printing	£325
Kenneth Anderson	Furniture	500
Margaret Blacklaws	Jewellery	500
Margery Clinton	Pottery	494
Anne Rhona Crichton	Weaving	500
Graham Crimmins	Jewellery	208
Hugh Falconer	Pottery	178
Glen Frame	Jewellery	500
Martin Glennie	Jewellery	435
Lionel Gliori	Musical instruments	500
Mike de Haan	Pottery	500
Margaret Hyne	Knitting and weaving	423
James Lockie	Loom making	237
Ian Massie	Jewellery	261
Vera Macdonald	Knitting	500
Sheena McLeod	Dolls	500
Andrew Naylor	Statuary	500
Nigel Picton	Wooden Toys	420
John Schofield	Woodturning	500
19		**£7981**

Name	Craft	Name
Sylvia Chalmers	Silk screen ptg.	Kevin Platt
John Deacons	Glass	George Constable
Selkirk Glass	Glass	Ian Johnstone
Anthony Mobbs	Jewellery	Michael Birnie
Eric Smith	Jewellery	Martin McGregor

1979-80

Name	Craft	Amount
Adlestrop	Furniture	£1146
Elizabeth Alston	Pottery	600
Eric Anderson	Pottery	678
Stanley Bonnar	Cast multiples	1146
Robert Crerar	Jewellery	1356
Hans Elleflaadt	Furniture	1146
Fiona Forder	Jewellery	1146
David Joy	Glass engraving	1356
Rankin & Linda Kinsman-Blake	Pottery	1146
Rachel Mackie *	Jewellery	1146
Heather Oswald	Knitting	840
Wendy Rae & Jennifer McLean *	Jewellery	900
Charles Ramsay	Glass	1146
Elizabeth Rowley	Stained glass	1356
Christine Smith	Pottery	1356
Heather Tosh	Pottery	1356
Bruce Walford/Fergus Stewart *	Pottery	1356
17		**£19176**

Name	Craft	Amount
John Butler	Weaving	£448
Bridget Drakeford	Pottery	500
Peter Fenton	Blacksmithing	500
Anne Clare Graham	Jewellery	500
David Gulland	Glass engraving	500
Anne Lightwood	Pottery	500
Denys Mitchell	Wrought ironwork	500
Zelda Mowat	Pottery	425
Jennifer Pettigrew	Batik	337
Sue & Tony Simpson	Leather	299
Eric Smith	Jewellery	326
Tim Stead	Furniture	500
John Strachan	Loom making	218
Ian Watt/Graham Halley	Musical inst.	500
14		**£6053**

Name	Craft	Name
Alan Hodgkinson	Jewellery	Guy Collins

1st April 1980 — 30th July 1980

Name	Craft	Amount
Anna Cady & Paul Clough	Weaving	£1356
Graeme Fleming	Pottery	1356
Chris Holmes *	Furniture	500
Gordon Lochhead	Bronze casting	672
Jane Robertson	Knitting	1356
Christopher Sharman	Leather	1356

Name	Craft	Amount
Susan Webster *	Jewellery	£1356
Kenneth Anderson	Furniture	500
David Kaplan	Glass	400
Diana Marshall	Knitting	195

Name	Craft	Name
Anne Clare Graham	Jewellery	Maxine Black
Jack Topen	Models	Paul Topen

*Denotes further grant

Crafts Commissioning Scheme

In existence since 1973, the Crafts Commissioning Scheme seeks to bring to the attention of a wide audience work produced by Scottish craftsmen. The scheme is administered on behalf of the Crafts Consultative Committee by the Scottish Craft Centre in Edinburgh.

The one major condition governing the acceptance of all commissions under the scheme is that the completed work should be seen by a wide public audience. Support and encouragement is normally given to specific projects related to new or existing buildings; pieces can also be produced for display in public collections.

Organisations such as public corporations, industries or business concerns and offices are eligible for assistance from the resources of the scheme. They might require a special presentation piece, a unique trophy or an important commemorative item. The work produced does not have to be specifically decorative, however, and it could be a series of functional pieces which could prove to be as inexpensive as mass produced goods, but with the especially attractive features of being designed for the client's needs alone and made with high quality workmanship.

Design competitions between several craftsmen are often used to aid the choice of a finished commission. In this way, more than one craftsman can benefit from the stimulus offered by a specific commission, and the completed work can be selected from several proposals, on the basis of quality and suitability. Wherever possible, the clients for a commission are encouraged to give a proportion towards the cost of a work, but this is not a prerequisite for assistance.

The scheme brings the work of Scottish craftsmen to the attention of people who might not otherwise realise the wealth of diverse and quality materials that can be hand-made in this country. It is hoped more and more companies and bodies will come to appreciate the potential of craft talent here in Scotland, thereby serving their own needs, and those of the craftsmen.

Highlands and Islands Development Board

The main responsibility for encouraging and assisting the development of craft activities in the Highlands and Islands of Scotland has been undertaken since 1965 by the Highlands and Islands Development Board. The Board, with headquarters in Inverness, was set up by Act of Parliament 'for the purpose of assisting the people of the Highlands and Islands to improve their economic and social conditions and of enabling the Highlands and Islands to play a more effective part in the economic and social development of the nation'. The area served by the Board — which has recently been slightly extended — comprises the Highland Region, the Western Isles, Shetland, Orkney, the District of Argyll and Bute, Arran and the Isles of Cumbrae.

The Board's services to the crafts industry include the provision of financial help towards the capital costs of setting up or expanding a business, the provision of factory or workshop accommodation on attractive financial terms, a comprehensive advisory and support service in the marketing field, and a range of other advisory services.

It is estimated that total sales of Highland craft products (excluding Shetland knitwear and Harris tweed) rose from about £350,000 in 1968 to £3.5M in 1975. No more recent estimate of aggregate sales is available; however, the Board approved financial assistance to 76 new crafts firms (most of them very small) during the period from 1975-1979 inclusive, whilst sales of existing crafts firms in the area continued to expand rapidly.

In 1970 the Board commissioned a study of gift and souvenir purchases by visitors to the Highlands and Islands. This showed that most visitors bought several separate items. The average expenditure of those interviewed was over £8, and it was established that visitors had a strong preference for products made in the area and were prepared to pay more for them. This finding led the Board in 1971 to launch its 'Craftmade' mark, which is promoted as guaranteeing the authentic Highland origin of the articles which carry the mark.

Also in 1970, the Board published a report on the Shetland Woolen Industry, produced by a specially constituted study group. This report recommended that a new Trade Mark should be designed and registered. Although the evidence suggests that the word 'Shetland', as applied to yarn and knitwear, is now regarded as a generic term in international usage, the Board felt that some benefit would accrue to the local knitwear industry from the establishment of a separate mark guaranteeing the geographical original of the garments. Accordingly, the Board established in 1972 a new Shetland Mark, which is now used by the majority of Shetland knitwear firms to promote the sales of their product.

Two other important elements in the Board's support for the marketing of craft products are the publication **Buyer's Guide to Retail Products of the Highlands and Islands** (now in its sixth edition) and its display centre in Church Street, Inverness. The display centre, which was opened in 1972, shares accommodation with the local tourist information centre, and contains an extensive exhibition of the area's craft products. Visitors are directed to local shops where they can buy the articles on display, and the centre handles over 10,000 enquiries per year.

Since 1971, the Board has organised an annual trade fair, known as the Highland Trade Fair, at Aviemore; this event, held in October, now attracts almost 200 exhibitors, most of whom are craft producers. The Board also helps crafts firms to exhibit at other suitable trade shows throughout the UK and sometimes abroad. To date, the Board has been involved in over 50 exhibitions on behalf of craft firms in the area.

As the new Highland Craftpoint organisation becomes fully operational, it will take over responsibility for providing training and technical services to craftsmen, and for the provision of industrial advice on design and marketing. The Board will retain responsibility for the following:

Financial help towards capital expenditure on business development

Help is usually provided in the form of grants and/or low-interest loans. Each case is individually considered by the Board on its merits, and craft firm proprietors are normally expected to raise about 50% of the project cost themselves. Exceptionally, this requirement may be relaxed to 30% particularly in remote rural areas.

Provision of factory/workshop accommodation

Advance or 'bespoke' factories or workshops can be made available by the Board on very attractive terms (including an initial rent-free period) for craft firms which offer prospects of employment for local people.

Collective marketing schemes

The Highland Trade Fair and other collective marketing schemes — including the publication of the Buyer's Guide and the administration of the Craftmade scheme — continue to be the Board's responsibility. Responsibility for marketing and other services to individual crafts firms will gradually be taken over by Highland Craftpoint.

Highland Craftpoint

Highland Craftpoint is a new company established in 1979 and jointly funded by the Highlands and Islands Development Board and the Scottish Development Agency. The company's function is to provide practical advice and assistance to craftsmen and crafts manufacturing firms throughout the Highlands and Islands, and in certain fields, in other parts of Scotland.

From the Autumn of 1980 Highland Craftpoint will be based in a purpose-built complex in the village of Beauly, a few miles north of Inverness. The complex has four special features: a library and information unit housing a comprehensive collection of books, slides and videotapes covering crafts design, methods and materials, as well as commercial practice for small firms and training methods; an exhibition unit presenting a series of exhibitions throughout the year, including work from other parts of the United Kingdom and overseas; a small conference unit and two three-thousand square foot workshops, one for precious metals and the other for ceramics, designed and equipped on small-scale production principles, providing for training, research and development, limited production and individual work.

Members of Highland Craftpoint's staff are appointed on the basis of their training and wide practical experience as craftsmen, designers and technicians. Practical advice of a direct kind, to meet clients' individual needs, will therefore be the central feature of the company's approach to its four main services: training, information, technical and marketing. Recognising the implications of time spent away from the workshop, these services are planned, wherever possible, to take place on a client's own premises. Senior staff, supported by visiting specialists, are available to discuss ideas, evaluate products and to conduct appraisals of equipment and workshop layouts, including manufacturing methods, on site. The workshops, library and other facilities at Beauly will be fully available to craftsmen to pursue individual research, supported and assisted by Highland Craftpoint staff.

Craft-based Firms

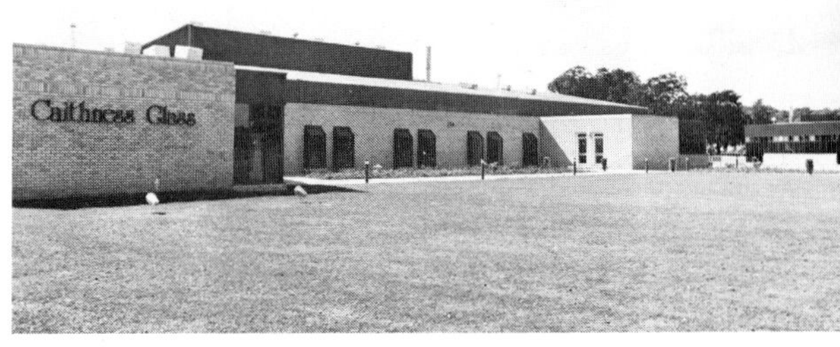

Crafts, to many people, mean individual, well designed and skillfully made objects manufactured in small and specialised workshops by master craftsmen. When not made to a commission, they are usually sold in galleries and specialist shops. For another sector of the public, crafts have a different and less appealing image: the gift or souvenir, sometimes proclaiming an ethnic origin, sold in quantity in tourist orientated gift shops. Much of this work is aimed at the lower end of the giftware market and to some people, crafts have — in many cases unjustifiably — become synonymous with cheap foreign imports from the Third World, or the heavily subsidised output of some Eastern Block countries.

These views encourage argument about the merit of individual or limited edition pieces compared with the output of craft based industries which use volume production methods. Undoubtedly some volume production 'crafted' products are deficient in design and finish, but this is by no means true in every case. The only real difference between the two categories is that one is designed to be capable of reproduction, whereas the other is designed specifically as a one-of-a-kind product. Each offers its own possibilities and limitations and equally, the standard can be high or low in both cases. Quality and value are not necessarily characteristics of unique objects any more than vulgarity and cheapness are features of the multiple.

In addition to its many flourishing workshops devoted to limited edition and individual pieces, Scotland has a significant presence of firms that work on a rather different basis: designs, manufacturing methods, skills and commercial attitudes aimed primarily at medium scale, volume production. This direction is not exclusive to any one craft, but is found equally in co-operatives of skilled hand and machine knitters, jewellers using casting methods and potters using jigger and jolley and slip casting techniques. The social contribution of enterprises such as Caithness Glass, Dust Jewellery, the Barbara Davidson Pottery and Highland Stoneware is evident in the opportunities they provide for skilled and satisfying employment at local level. Their contribution to the national economy is undeniable: firms of this type generate a significant part of the several millions of pounds annually earned by the Scottish crafts industry. In purely aesthetic terms, a proportion of volume production 'crafted' products are of merit, by any standard.

The fundamental characteristic of a firm of this type is market awareness, and a willingness to design to meet its demands. By conventional craft workshop standards they will probably work from larger premises, using more substantial equipment — some of it may be quite sophisticated — and will employ more staff. They are also likely to spend more on research and development, and will certainly devote more time, energy and money to marketing and advertising. As their investment and employment obligations will be relatively large, their ability to be aware of and responsive to the market is essential. Far from implying a loss of integrity by their principals — who in the four cases that follow, had backgrounds as trained designer craftsmen in the conventional sense — the need for market orientation, as opposed to a more simple and personal desire to make, has clearly acted as a positive artistic stimulus and intellectual challange.

Founded in 1960, Caithness Glass has an international reputation for its distinctive glassware. From its original base in Wick in Caithness, the company has established further factories at Oban and Perth producing between them a wide range of glass tableware and decorative pieces. It is particularly well known for its paperweights and almost 200 different designs have been produced since 1969. Caithness Glass is probably the largest craft based firm in Scotland, employing over 200 people, many of them drawn from locally recruited school leavers, who follow the company's own comprehensive training programme. Some make glass — all of its products are mouth blown — while others work as glass engravers using copper-wheel, diamond-point and sand-blasting techniques. Like many successful craft based firms, Caithness Glass covers both volume production as well as limited editions and special one-of-a-kind pieces, such as the well known 'Mastermind' television trophy.

Dust Jewellery was the brainchild of former Grays's School of Art student Norman Grant, who began making jewellery in a small garden shed in 1967. By 1970 he employed one person, exhibited at one trade fair and sold 80% of his output in Scotland. In 1980, the company will exhibit at seven British and European trade fairs, sells only 7% of its work in Scotland and employs 30 people in a purpose-built workshop. In addition to its main base in Lundin Links, it is involved with another Scottish jewellery firm, has a retail outlet in Edinburgh, a London office and a sister company, Dust Graphics. This pace and scale of development has come about from combining technical innovations — particularly in the fields of enamel and photoetching — with a vigorous marketing policy. Investment in sophisticated equipment and operating on a broad design and manufacturing base have contributed to the company's success and survival in a highly competitive field.

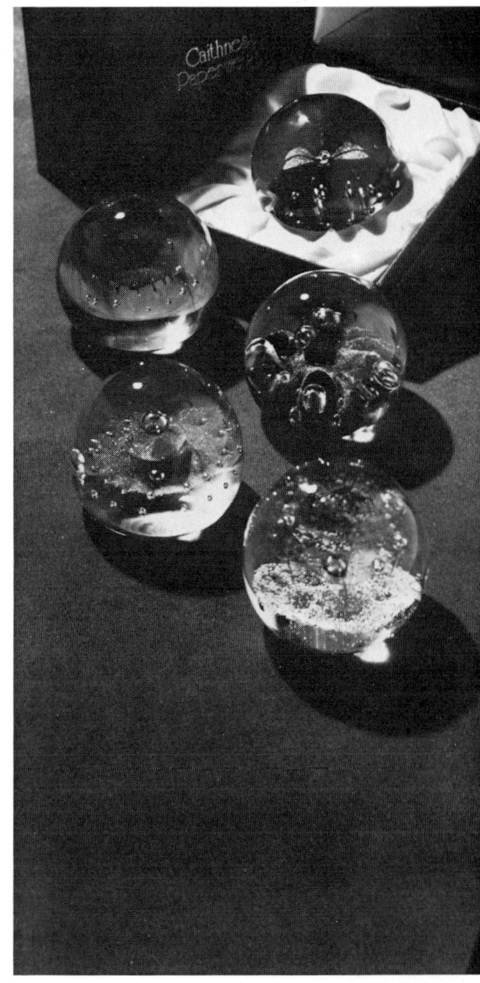

A selection of Highland Stoneware
tableware.
Highland Stoneware workshops.

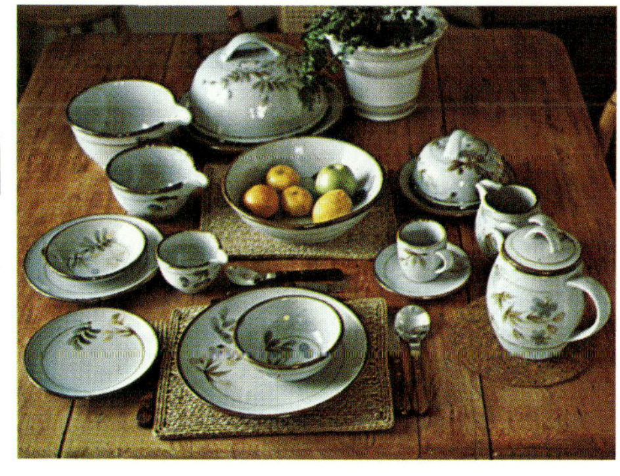

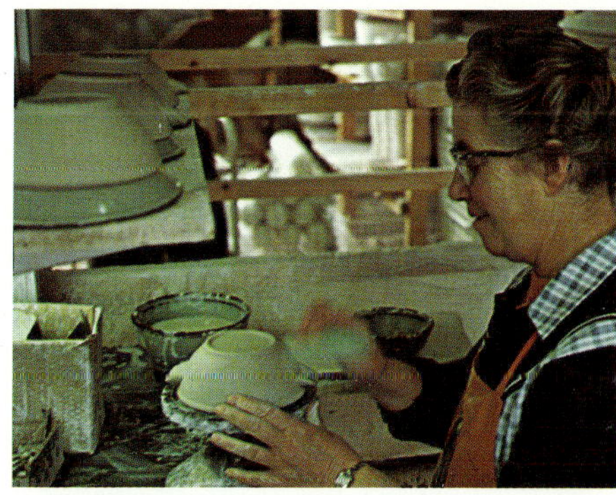

The Barbara Davidson Pottery began in similarly humble circumstances: a rented byre and home-made potter's wheel worked in evenings and at weekends. As a result of public interest in their work, Barbara and Brian McLuckie gave up their full time jobs — as art teacher and engineer, and devoted all of their time to pottery. Since 1972 the company has worked from a converted farmhouse and outbuildings, and currently employs 25 staff producing a wide range of tableware made by a combination of semi-industrial methods with hand finishing and decorating. The use of up-to-date equipment enables the pottery to achieve efficient and economic production, while a recently introduced computerised record system aids administration and helps order processing for customers in the UK, Europe, North America and Scandinavia. But there are two sides to its production: one, called Larbert Pottery, employs semi-industrial methods while the other, the Barbara Davidson Pottery is exclusively concerned with handmade work produced by Barbara and two assistants.

Pottery, compared with jewellery, is a low value yet high freight product, and it is surprising to learn just how many potters choose to operate their businesses from locations that are often remote from both a source of raw materials and their markets. For a pottery devoted to medium scale volume production, using jigger and jolley methods, to locate itself in a relatively remote West Highland location might seem the height of folly, but in the case of Highland Stoneware, the gamble has been successful. The company's prototypes, developed jointly by David Grant and Royal College tutor Graham Clarke, were designed specifically for quantity production, and focussed on a co-ordinated range of tableware made in high quality reduced stoneware. The suitability of shapes was tested on small production runs, then refined, and the results market tested in carefully selected outlets. Only after this, was the range launched. The company's success is in no small part due to the logic of its approach as well as its design, production and marketing policy. The combination produces a quality product made by local people, hand decorated to a high standard, and sold to prestigious outlets throughout the UK and Europe.

Scale, resources and output place these four firms, and others like them, in a position between that of the one or two man workshop and large scale industry. Products can be made to a keen price and will inevitably achieve wider distribution than would be possible for the output of a small workshop. Public acceptance of well designed and made craft based products can lead to interest in exclusive items, in addition to making a wider range of quality products available to the discriminating consumer. Their position also gives them an advantage over large scale industry, particularly in the fields of ceramics and jewellery where the combination of manpower, traditional specialisation and job demarcation, as well as the sheer level of capital investment involved inhibits industry's capacity for innovation. The successful craft based firm on the other hand, has an inbuilt capacity for innovation, flexible working methods and a team spirit to match. They invariably are led by someone who is personally capable of carrying out most, if not all, of the techniques involved to a high level. The consequent benefits to Scottish craftsmanship and its technology, the economy and the consumer are considerable.

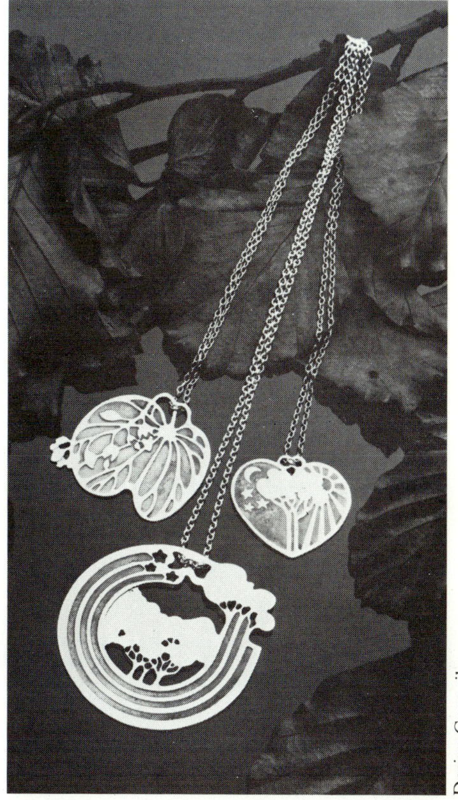

Norman Grant jewellery.

Larbert Pottery "clouds" a selection of
finished clouds tableware.

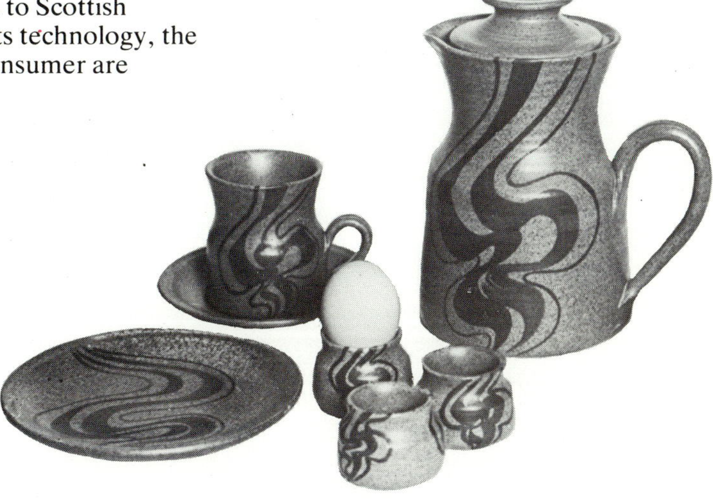

A selection of Caithness Glass
paperweights.

acid-etch: decorating glass by etching with hydroflouric acid through a resist (*q.v.*).

acrylic: glass-clear tough and light plastics material (polymethylmethacrylate) available in many colours and adopted recently by jewellers; it can be moulded or cut.

anodised: aluminium after oxidation in an acid bath can be coloured by immersion in dye; designs can be created by stopping off areas. Anodised decoration is not generally sunproof.

arras: *see* tapestry

bisque: unglazed white porcelain or, any pottery which has been given a preliminary firing before glazing to facilitate this operation.

chase: modelling the surface of metal with hammers and punchers.

coil: handbuilding pots from rolls of clay smoothed together.

copper-wheel engraving: decorating glass by grinding it against the lower edge of a rotating copper wheel over which an abrasive is fed in a stream of water.

cuir bouilli: leather, softened in boiling water, stretched over a core, then hardened by drying. Boxes and vessels so formed are decorated by tooling (*q.v.*)

diamond-point engraving: decorating glass by scratching and stippling with a diamond or steel pointed tool.

dobby loom: loom whose shafts, which control the movement of the warp (*q.v.*) threads, are raised according to a pattern chain of pegged wooden slats. The pegs can be changed and set to enable weaving of complicated patterns.

Fair-isle: decorative bands of geometric pattern knitted in several colours, often on the wrists and neck of pullovers, which originated in Fair Isle and Shetland.

glaze: a mixture of silica, fluxes (which melt the silica) alumina (to stiffen the runny silica) and water, into which pots are dipped before final firing, to make them non-porous. Glaze is often coloured by the addition of metal oxides.

gobelin: *see* tapestry.

gouache: watercolour painting with opaque colours mixed with honey and gum.

hemming: doubling over and sewing down the border of a garment to conceal the raw edge of cloth.

high-loom: *see* tapestry.

jigger and jolley: a method of making repitition shapes, such as cups and plates, on the potter's wheel using plaster mould and jigs.

lustre: film-like coating of metallic oxide added to an already-glazed pot and fired again at a lower temperature to produce a shiny, metallic effect.

milling: passing sheet metal through rollers to make it of a thinner gauge.

pontil rod: metal rod used to handle glass during manufacture. It leaves a round depression.

press-moulding: making shapes by pressing sheets of clay into plaster moulds. Handles and spouts are often press-moulded.

porcelain: translucent, white and very hard china clay which fires at a high temperature. Discovered in China in the seventh century A.D. it was not made in Europe until the eighteenth century.

purfling: decorating the edge of a stringed musical instrument with inlaid wood.

raku: method of firing pots at a low temperature, taking them from the still hot kiln and either plunging them into water or rolling them in some organic combustible material. Pots so produced have a characteristically crackled glaze. They were originally made in Japan for the tea-drinking ceremony.

resist: substance painted on cloth, metal or pottery to inhibit or 'stop' dye adhering; wax is frequently used and removed by heating after the dying process.

Roman: in calligraphy, monumental capitals based on the lettering used by the Romans on Trajan's column.

sand-blasting: decorating glass by blasting the surface with an air-jet carrying fine particles of corundum or chilled steel: this produces an opaque effect. Areas to be left clear can be masked with tape or wire. (For safety reasons sand is not now generally used.)

setting and finishing: handwoven cloth for garments must be set to give dimensional stability and a controlled elasticity, to prevent it bagging in wear. It is steamed and ironed. Woolen yarn containing oil and dirt must then be scoured by washing and drying on a slatted roller. Certain heavy clothes need to be shrunk by being worked ('waulked') in a soap solution before rinsing and drying.

sgraffito: decorating pottery by dipping it into liquid clay of a different colour and scratching through this to reveal the body of the pot.

shaft: wood or metal frame suspended in a loom to keep taut the heddles, wires through an eye in which the warp threads pass. The shafts can be raised or lowered to form an opening in the warp for the passage of the weft thread.

sinnet: a sort of flat, braided cordage.

slab-building: handbuilding pots from sheets of clay which can be joined as in woodworking to make hard-edged form.

slip-casting: making pots by pouring liquid clay (slip) into plaster of Paris moulds.

steel-point engraving: *see* diamond-point.

stop: *see* resist.

table loom: small, loom designed to be easily transportable.

tapestry: weft-face woven fabric in which the different coloured wefts are not thrown to the full width of the warp but manipulated into patterns. Also known as arras or gobelin from early, famous Continental manufactories, it is usually worked on a high loom, where the warp threads are vertically suspended and the tapestry design or cartoon can be transferred on to the warp threads.

tooled: decorated leather, often for book-binding, worked with brass punches. The impressions may be gilt or left blind, that is ungilt.

uncial: a form of majuscule script with large round characters, originally used in fourth to eighth century Classical manuscripts.

vellum: very durable writing and book-binding material prepared from calf skin treated with lime and polished.

warp: threads which stretch the length of a woven cloth. They can show, on warp-face material, or be covered by the weft.

weft: threads which run across woven cloth from edge to edge and pass through the warp threads. If they conceal the warp, the fabric is known as weft-face.